Skills to Critical Thinking

A Self-Help Book for Parents and Teachers

By

Donald J. Dickinson

Heart-Whitlow Publishers, 1845 Brandywine Dr., Lenoir City, TN 37772
http://skillstocriticalthinking.com

Skills to Critical Thinking:
A Self-Help Book for Parents and Teachers

ISBN 978-0-9637951-0-6

Subjects: Critical Thinking/Education/Parenting/Teaching/Instruction/Psychology

Manuscript preparation by Cripple Beagle Publishing, Jody Dyer, editor.

Dedication

This book is dedicated to the graduate students from the *University of Tennessee, Department of Educational Counseling and Psychology,* who performed parent training with me starting as early as 1973, where they trained individual parents to improve their children's learning. Many students whose parents were trained probably faced school with more success because of the willingness of their parents to take part in tutoring their children. Also, thanks to those graduate students who conducted workshops for parents, made convention presentations, helped develop the *Easy Reading Books,* and did research on parent training and cognitive learning.

Acknowledgements

Without the constant feedback and editing of this book from my cousin Sylvia Jackson, it would probably never have been finished. Her assistance is much appreciated, and I could never repay her. Also, thanks to the parents who read and provided feedback on the manuscript over several years, and special thanks goes to Ms. Annietta Unruh, Home-school Coordinator, Knoxville Christian School. She was the first parent to read the manuscript and provide a chapter by chapter rating with comments that were exceptionally helpful. Also, very helpful was the evaluation by Ms. Kathy Millusick, who was the last parent to view the manuscript and who provided detailed feedback and communicated with me on making corrections to the manuscript. Don and Barbara Pardue were always ready to read a chapter without delay. Thanks, Don and Barbara.

Also, many thanks are given to teachers who viewed the manuscript and especially Christina Bridges Rodriquez, who wrote a 10-page evaluation and corresponded with me after she implemented some of the suggestions for teaching critical thinking. I also thank the teachers at Midway Elementary School for letting me observe their teachers teaching critical thinking.

I also appreciate the assistance of Dr. Lori Schmeid, whose most recent book is *History of Neuroscience*. She was kind enough to review my comments about how the brain processes information and to offer corrections. Also, Ms. Jody Dyer, editor of *Cripple Beagle Publishing Company,* gave me encouragement, made suggestions, and read and corrected many parts of the manuscript. Your work was appreciated.

Last but not least, this book would have never been finished without the help of my wife, Teresa Ann, whose prefrontal cortex, which is necessary for reasoning and judgment, is much stronger than mine causing me to defer to her when there was some ambiguity as to what I should say. Thanks Teresa.

Chapters

Figures

Chapter 1
Parents and Teachers Together

Haven't you heard it said, "He's just like his dad?" You know why, don't you? It's because dad is a teacher . . . like it or not . . . and for better or worse. And mom and dad also become the teachers of knowledge. They do it by teaching words to reason and think with. They teach concepts like big and small and up and down. They teach their children facts, like their names, their addresses, their phone numbers, and birthdays. And before their children are off to school, parents teach their youngsters the skills that build the ability to think critically. Then it's time for the teachers to take the lead in teaching critical thinking. Chapter1 introduces some of the skills that are required for critical thinking and gives you an idea of how together parents and teachers can teach critical thinking.

Although teachers are the primary teachers of critical thinking, parents might be surprised to know that they could be most effective. Yes, if parents start early, they could be more effective than some teachers or college professors. By the time your youngsters team up with college professors, it may be a little too late. Parents can and do teach critical thinking, although it may be only some of the components, and they do it right after their children start to walk—like teaching their children such concepts as "bye" and "thank you." These concepts will be added to their knowledge to help them do critical thinking at a later date. (Yes, knowledge is an important factor in critical thinking.) You don't teach critical thinking all at one time; you teach it year after year as your children advance with age, and it is taught with the help of parents, teachers, media, books, and other resources.

Stop for a moment to think of all the decisions that your children will face in the future. If your children are ruled by habits and act without considering all the factors, they will behave like robots being controlled by peers, television, videos, and what they read—without ever considering the implications. That is dangerous, because they will be faced with such important decisions as using drugs, choosing friends, eating healthy, choosing occupations, deciding to have a designer baby (genetically altering hair or eye color, height, skeleton) or not, to get the very most out of their educations or to just pass, to taking care of their planet earth . . . and even life-threatening events that you cannot imagine now.

In her book *The Witches* (about the Salem witch trials), Stacy Schiff describes the dilemma you and your children *currently face*: "We all prescribe to preposterous beliefs; we just don't know yet which ones they are. We often have been known to prefer plot to truth; to deny the evidence before us in favor of the ideas behind us; to do insane things in the name of reason . . . ." Critical thinking will allow your youngsters to evaluate and question ideas instead of accepting them at face value. Most of all: they will need to evaluate their own ideas, knowledge, and beliefs. They certainly will need some critical-thinking skills in order to manage the future.

Don't Wait until Their Brains are Fully Developed

Don't think you need to wait until your children's brains are fully developed to start teaching critical thinking. Sure, the part of the brain (prefrontal cortex) that is most often thought to be responsible for critical thinking is not completely developed until children pass through adolescence, but if you wait that long, you're going to have some big trouble teaching your children to become effective critical thinkers. Critical thinking is not some big, wrapped-up skill that you teach in a formal course in high school; instead it *has skills* or parts that fit together to make your children effective thinkers.

Brian Christian and Tom Griffiths, authors of *Algorithms to Live By* ask, "Why are four-year-olds, for instance, still better than million-dollar supercomputers at a host of cognitive tasks, including vision, language, and causal reasoning?" If your children can outthink a million-dollar supercomputer, you can certainly teach some thinking skills.

The *skills presented in this book* start early in the life of your youngsters and are taught by family. As the children become older and start school, teachers join with parents to impart these skills. There is no skipping a skill; because all skills are important . . . each is essential but not sufficient by itself to cause your youngsters to become critical thinkers.

But teachers already teach the skills to critical thinking

Teachers get a great deal of flack when they are accused of not teaching critical thinking. Certainly, they may not teach each and every single component required for thinking critically at one time, but you can rest assured that they teach many of the skills for critical thinking and have been teaching these for years and years as your children advance through the grades.

But if anything is missing in what they teach, it would be the teaching of an *objective attitude* regardless of past learning, beliefs, and biases. And children must be taught to recognize that their thinking habits must be scrutinized. *It is as important for them to question their own thinking as it is to question the thinking of others*. That requires learning to be open to new information, seeking the best answers while knowing that these best answers can change. Parents are also remiss in teaching this step.

Then there's another component: your children should be able to reason effectively with the information they have, to put information in order to clarify the problem, the evidence, the arrival at a *thoughtful conclusion* while resisting the kneejerk tendency to jump to a conclusion. They must identify exactly what the problem is and what is implied if it is not stated. They need to note the evidence for the problem, scrutinize it for accuracy, and seek additional information if necessary to see if it is valid. In other words, they must identify the evidence before arriving at a conclusion. If there is no explicit evidence they must use implicit information to make an inference about the validity of the premise. That's sometimes called "connecting the dots." Parents, how often do you use these skills with your children? Some parents do and some don't. All should.

Baby skills

Parents, you actually teach some components of critical thinking before your babies get a year old. You're getting your children ready for school from the time they are born to the time they pass through the schoolhouse doors . . . and you should keep it up until their brains reach full maturity. When your babies are born they have 100 billion neurons. As a result of environmental stimulation, these neurons make trillions of connections. If connections are not used, their brains are "pruned" of those not used. So parents should take advantage of the critical period for developing some cognitive skills. Keep in mind the children have excitable brain activity like no other they will experience when they get older. This excitable brain makes learning come faster and last longer. Suzanne Bouffard, in her book *Most Important Years,* says that children's brains develop at a much faster rate during pre-K years than at any time in their lives. Parents, don't miss a chance to help your children to grow the foundation for a lifetime of higher learning.

The first step toward critical thinking with your children is baby skills

Yes, you use baby skills when you start teaching the first instructional skills of critical thinking. Children learn concepts right away. They learn all kinds of *concrete* concepts, like chair, table, car, dish, wagon, and fork. They also learn a number of *abstract* concepts like what's big and little, yes and no, fast and slow, and up and down. Since they like to be picked "up" and will let you know it, it follows that they then learn concept rules (how concepts are arranged) like "up," "me," and "pick." This later comes to be "Pick me up" and is a grammar arrangement of verb, pronoun, and preposition. You can see they are learning grammar before they are three years old.

There's no reasoning without words—at least for most humans.

Parents are also responsible for teaching words, and most of us use words to reason. Just try reasoning without using words. The more words your youngsters know, the better they will be able to learn to read. With more words, they can more clearly express their thinking. The more words they know, the better they will know what you are saying and be able to understand their teachers when they start to school.

It's never too late to start teaching critical thinking

Although adults and adolescents have less brain cell as when they were children, they still have plenty to learn to think critically. In fact, more mature adults have brains that have fully developed capacity in the frontal cortex which is the area of the brain used to reasons critically.

Critical thinking in college students can be improved by their taking a single course in college that *focuses on a few skills* of critical thinking. Even practicing debating can improve critical thinking. So it's never too late, but children could be more effective thinkers if the teaching had started earlier. Parents should join hand in hand with teachers in showing their children not to jump to conclusions and not to see all things as black or white with no shades of gray. By working jointly, both demonstrating critical thinking and both providing evidence for their views, then all skills can be effectively taught to older children. (Spouses, don't give up on your mates; it's never too late.)

Many Skills to Critical Thinking

There are *two main types of skills* that are used in critical thinking. One is the *learning of basic skills* and the second is *using what you have learned* in an effective manner. The first one is called *knowledge* and the second is called *metacognitive* skills or simply "using your head." These latter skills are used for monitoring and evaluating your thinking as you use the knowledge you have acquired.

Skills to knowledge

Knowledge is all that information and experience you have stored in your memory banks. This includes information you may have learned in school like parts of the nervous system, the structure of the human cell, or how to add and subtract, but it also includes experiences—like how to please your sister or get the dog to bark. You use this knowledge in problem solving and critical thinking.

Your children learn this information by learning the basic skills of concepts, facts, comprehension, practice, and how to make corrections. These are similar to study skills, only many of these skills can be applied directly to critical thinking and reasoning. These skills will help fill your children's heads with all kind of information that can be used to think critically. Your children just can't reason unless they have some information to reason with. You can't determine the reasons for WWI without knowing something about WWI.

Skills to using your head

Think of *knowledge* and *using your head* to be like a computer. You put information (knowledge) like names, addresses, ages, experience, or education into the computer. Once the information is entered, you are able to use the information to answer questions like, "What is the average age and education of the people whose information has been entered?" You could even ask how many people are named "Bob" or "Betty." You brain is just like that; you need information in your head so you can now use it to solve problems and think critically.

Skills to reasoning

There are many kinds of reasoning (cause-and-effect, deductive, inductive, classification, and so on) and these can be taught in early elementary school and by parents. Try this example with a preschool child. Show them a coin and tell them you want them to figure out which hand the coin is in. Emphasize it will be in one hand or the other. Put your hands behind your back and let the child guess which hand the coin is in. If the child guesses the wrong hand, they will obviously pick the other hand. It "stands to reason" that if the statement is true that the coin is in one hand or the other, then if it is not in the left hand, it therefore must be in the right hand. This is called *reasoning by elimination*. Children learn from experience to do this kind of reasoning early in life. When children make mistakes, they can reason by comparing their answer to a correct example. This called *reasoning by example* and can be taught to children in elementary school.

Skills Based on How Your Brains Work

This book provides parents and teachers with some methods for teaching children the skills to critical thinking, and with the learning of these skills, they can make better decisions about learning life skills. These skills are based on how your children's brains work when they learn and retrieve information, when they are upset, when they problem-solve, and when they dream, to mention a few . . . and the rules given to you in this book are based on contemporary brain science. Yes, that's right! You can learn how to change your children's brains. We know a stimulating environment can alter your youngster's brains, that teaching certain skills can change their brains, and that even *prompting* them to change their moods can change their brains *and* their mood. We've come a long way in learning the connection between learning and brain anatomy.

So You Don't Have Time to Teach Critical Thinking

So you don't have time to teach critical thinking to your children—even though it is one of the most important cognitive skills you could ever teach them; it could even be a life or death skill. Your children will be faced with a world tittering on a nuclear disaster, extreme weather events never seen before, and our democracy threatened by social media. Robots already control our thinking on your smart phone so they can increase the time you use these electronic devices.

If you ever want to leave a legacy to your descendents, teach your children critical thinking so they can pass the skills and abilities on to their children and their children will pass it on to their children and thus this will be passed on for generation to generation. If you want to leave a legacy that could last decades, you will find that the teaching of critical thinking will be appreciated through the generations. What a legacy!

Alright, parents you have family responsibilities and perhaps a job and have difficulty just getting everyone off to work or school each day. Okay teachers, you have all those objectives to meet and tests to measure them that you are overwhelmed. If you don't meet the standards, your salary might be in jeopardy, maybe even your job.

But parents and teacher can still teach critical thinking when doing the house or yard work, or going to church, or the movies, or the lake for a swim or even while teaching algebra or social studies. All you need to do is model (demonstrate) how to think critically with the tasks you already do. Then have your children demonstrate that they have learned from your demonstration and make corrections if necessary. That's all there is to it . . . except you must first know and be able to demonstrate the skills to critical thinking.

This is a self-help book

Consider that you want to teach your children how to become critical thinkers and to reason logically. Just how are you going to teach them unless you know the skills yourself? Assume you are going to teach your child how to tie her shoes. How could you do this is you don't know how to tie your own shoes. You couldn't. Consequently, this book is for parents and teachers as well as for their youngsters. In order for you to become competent in critical thinking, you must do everything yourself that you will ask your students to do.

You will not passively read this book, but like your children, you will answer questions, capture the essence of what has been presented, organize your thinking for better comprehension, and practice for improving long-term memory. That means that you, as parents and teachers, must also be *active learners* as you move through the skills to critical thinking. Have a note pad or some way of taking notes because you will need it starting with the next chapter.

Summary/ Essence

A summary should contain the important concepts and the supporting concepts of a passage. The summary should also contain the essence—the most important or basic parts of a reading or lecture. They are different. A summary may list all that was covered while the essence is something you believe is the heart and soul of the reading. It's important to you! An example will be given in the next chapter including how to make notes.

Also, make certain your notes are precise and concise. Children should select the most import parts of the chapter and make notes. I have found an inverse relationship between the length of students' notes in my classes and how they do on an exam. When they write too much they have more to review, the more likely they are to make mistakes, and the longer it takes for them to study. You will see another example of precise and concise notes in the next chapter.

Reward Yourself

There are parts of your brain that are sometimes called the pleasure centers. When you stimulate these areas, you are likely to repeat what you did to stimulate them in the first place. When rats who were trained to press levers to get food or water found that they could press a third lever to get an electrical stimulation of their brain's pleasure centers, it was so stimulating that they would ignore the food and water until they collapsed from pressing the level that stimulated their brains.

Now, intelligent machines have used the same method of stimulating your brains to get you and your children "hooked" on using their machines. Take for instance the smart phone apps. If technicians want to increase the time you use your smart phone, all they need to do is catch you using the phone and give you something that stimulates your pleasure centers. Does it work? Yes, indeed. The average number of times you or your children check your phones every day is 47, and the average number of hours spent on your smart phones if five. (It is also known that excessive use of electronic devises decreases learning in school. Does your child average five hours studying each day?)

What they give you and your children to keep you looking is *either positive feedback, social approval, or a sense of progress.* What if this same technology is used in this book to keep you studying in the most effect way so you can become a super teacher of critical thinking to your youngsters? Wouldn't that be more beneficial than heavy use of your cell phones?

In the *next five chapters*, you will record your progress and will receive some positive feedback for how you are *performing against a standard.* You will be recording *how well you followed the rules for learning* that are researched based, and these rules for learning can be applied to the learning of other subject matters. (You will be learning how to learn.)You can use this technique with your children too.

(The words *children* and *students* are used interchangeably in this book.)

Chapter 2
Learning Basic Comprehension

Have you understood everything that has been presented in this book so far? If the answer is "yes," you were probably using your comprehension skills. These are the same skills you will need to teach your children. However, if you did not understand everything you have read so far, you will need to learn a few comprehension skills—like trying to understand every sentence; if you still do not understand every sentence, then reread (and think about the sentence.) If you still don't get it, you should go back and look at the context or heading; and if you still don't understand, look for examples. If your mind is still blank, you should then go to the internet, use a dictionary, encyclopedia, and books, or consult someone who might be able to explain the text. Doing that would be good start on comprehension, but there's more. Don't forget: comprehension is a skill that is essential for thinking critically. You're going to read about basic reading comprehension in this chapter and deeper comprehension in the next chapter. Please have a notebook handy for taking notes as you read this chapter and start using the steps mentioned above.

Key Words:
Schemata
Instructional level
Meaningful
Key words

(Key words are words you should know before or learn as you read this chapter. Look for them as you read what follows.)

Q: What are the most important *first steps* for critical thinking?
Q: What are the rules for teaching the first steps in comprehending?

This is Important! It's Going to be on Your Test

Your teachers may have told you time and time again, "This is important; it's going to be on your test!" That's why you have questions at the beginning of each chapter in this book. The questions tell you *what look for as you read each chapter* because they are *important*. They're going to be on the test. *When you finish reading each chapter, you should be able to answer the questions.* This works—you'll learn more—so please do it.

Comprehension is necessary to think critically

Assume you are given a legal document charging your client with destroying a person's property. His attorney has sent you a copy of this legal document. You need to use the rule for critical thinking as you read it like identifying exactly what the problem is, what is the evidence, is the evidence base on objective data, and what are the qualifications of the personal making the claims? As you read the document you must comprehend what you are reading so you use the simple rules mentioned in the introduction like trying to understand every sentence and re-reading when you cannot understand it. These are basic rules should be followed whether it is a legal document of reading a text for a school assignment.

You Can Teach Comprehension

Parents often are faced with this situation: *Mr. Smith: But my child's problem is that he reads something and can't answer the* questions *about what he has just read. How can I correct this? It's not like correcting a math problem where I just show him how to do it.*

Parents are befuddled by this situation all the time. How in the world do you teach children to comprehend what they just read or what you have just told them? Many parents think that children just need to be smart or mature enough to do this. However, reading comprehension can be taught by a few simple steps that will be discussed in this chapter and the next.

Comprehension is a concept that is difficult to define because it's an abstract concept. Here a definition of comprehension that will be used in this chapter: *To comprehend means to understand or to construct meaning with what has been presented and to connect the presentation with one's prior knowledge.* It means *finding the essence* of what has been read or said and being able to make an inference from information that is not explicit. Wow! That's a lot of big words. What exactly do these words mean? You may tell youngsters you want them to comprehend, construct meaning, or find the essence, but they may not understand what these words mean. These are abstract concepts. So you need to also teach these concepts and provide examples that they can understand. Look for examples of comprehension as you read this chapter.

A First Step for Comprehending

Here are some simple rules to follow to improve reading comprehension; some of these steps would also apply to hearing a presentation. They may sound simple, and they are, but they can have a profound influence on your children's learning if they will use them. Attempt to get your students motivated to follow the steps for comprehending. Can you do it? You tell them how important it is and that they learn a great deal more. Persuade them, prompt them, and even beg them if you must. Will this work? Let's see if it works on you as you, too, should follow these steps if you are going to be a good model for your children.

- Try to understand every sentence in a reading assignment. (When you come to words you do not know, use your laptop or other electric device to look up the meaning of the word.) Sometimes you will need to concentrate on several lines or even a paragraph in order to understand a concept.
  - Reread the sentence when you do not understand it.
  - Look for examples to help to understand the concept or the context of what has been said.
  - Look for captions and titles as a clue for what is being said.
  - If the sentence or paragraph is a long one, break it into parts and try to understand one part at a time.
    Look up every word you do not know in the sentence or

paragraph.

- If these steps do not work, ask for help. This is important. You learn by asking questions, so ask.

      If you are now asking yourself, "Is that all there is to it?" Well, the answer is "not by a long shot," because your kids can follow these rules until they are blue in the face and still not have success they need. What follows are some of the reasons why they may have difficulty and how to make the reading material so your children will succeed.

Before You Start

 Before you start demonstrating (demonstrating is the same as modeling) to your children how to comprehend, there are several steps you should take to make certain that your *students have the prerequisites to comprehend the "material" you intend to teach them.* Your children's *background, vocabulary, and reading ability* all have an impact on comprehension.

Figure 1   Comprehension

Types of
Skills that influence reading comprehension

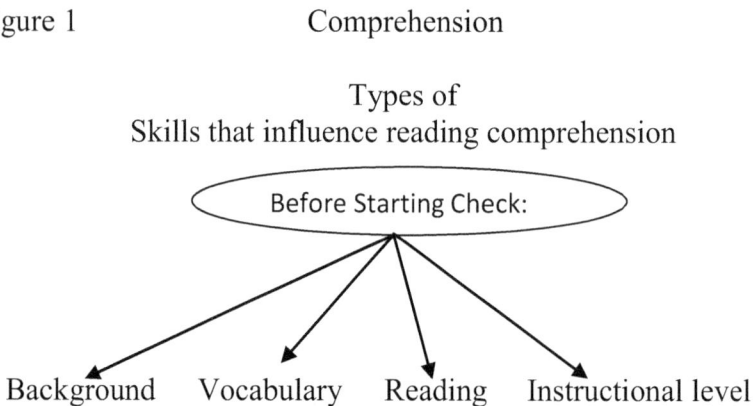

Background   Vocabulary   Reading   Instructional level

Before you start trying to teach comprehension, make certain your students have the background, vocabulary, can read, and the material is at an instructional level.

Background

Background *is having experiences similar to what is being studied.* An auto mechanic may have a background with several Hondas, but when a new model comes out, the manual may allude to new concepts he has never seen before. Because of his past experience with similar cars, he is able to figure out what the new parts do. A person with a background in ancient literature might not do as well. One way to help your children understand their reading material is by selecting the *key words* in the material and reviewing them with your students so they will better comprehend the lesson.

Vocabulary

We already know there is a strong relationship between children's reading comprehension and their vocabulary. As their vocabulary goes up, so does reading comprehension and vice-versa. Hart and Risley, in their book entitled *Meaningful Differences*, report that, by age 3, children from homes of professional parents have heard *30 million words* compared to children of working-class parents who have heard only *10 million* words. *Children of upper class families spend 60 percent less time watching television* than lower class families and have more quality verbal interactions with their parents. All this results in a larger vocabulary for upper-class students and more success in school over the working-class children. So you must make certain there is a *match between your students' vocabulary and "the material" that you are using for instruction.* In general, the larger the children's vocabularies, the better their comprehension.

Example of fit between the student's vocabulary and the reading assignment

Assume a high-school teacher plans to use a short story by Vincent Sheean about Winston Churchill for an English Literature class. After determining the reading rate is average for her students, the teacher then needs to check to see if students have a sufficient vocabulary to comprehend the story.

First, the teacher should peruse the story looking for words that might be too difficult. Some words are more important than others, like "valediction," which is in the title. If the teacher had already read the story, the most critical words (key words) for comprehending could be identified. If any students have difficulty with 10 to 15 percent of the words, the teacher should teach the meaning of the words before having the students read the selection. Here's an example of how a parent might do this:

Parent: When you read from your book, you read at a rate of 92 words per minute with only a couple of errors. Nice going! Now we need to see if you know the meaning of several words in the story.

Parent: Tell me the meaning of *arduous*? (Reads word in a sentence.)

Student: I think that means something outrageous.

Parent: Alright, what is the meaning of the word *aesthetic*? (Reads word in a sentence.)

Student: To be a good athlete.

This illustration shows that although reading rate and error rate are acceptable, students can still have difficulty understanding a reading assignment simply because they do not understand many of the words in the assignment.

Example of vocabulary for preschool children

Parents and preschool teachers should help children develop vocabulary skills. Children love to be read to at an early age. Such classic stories as *Snow White and the Seven Dwarfs, Cinderella*, and *Beauty and the Beas*t are all-time favorites of children. But take a look at a *Little Golden Book* vocabulary in the first paragraph of the first page of *Beauty and the Beast*. Such words as *prince* and *castle* are used in the first sentence and are not known by most three-year olds who none-the-less love this story. (These are *key words* that your children should know or you should teach them early in the story.) In the second paragraph the words of *shelter* and *repulsed* were used, and this story goes on and on with advanced words.

These are important words, but your children might be overwhelmed if you try to teach each and every word as you read the story. Substitute words that mean the same that the children might know, and after reading the story several times, start to explain some of the words while not slowing down the story too much.

Reading

A child's reading skill level is another issue that may present difficulty during comprehension exercises. It is obvious that if your children cannot read the material, they will not be able to understand what is presented. Before starting to teach how to comprehend, check your pupils to determine if the material you are using is too difficult for them to read at an instructional level. You can do this by photocopying a page of their reading book. Use the photocopy to record their reading accuracy. Don't count the small stuff like omitting the past tense or plurals or inserts (you can do this later). Have them read for two minutes while noting their errors. Ideally, they should miss no more than 10 percent of the words in order to maintain a high level of motivation, although a lower level of errors would be desirable.

Questions within a Lesson

It may surprise you to know that answering questions within a section can increase your comprehension. That's why I include questions in every chapter of this book. Answering questions *within* a lesson doubles your learning compared to answering no questions or answering questions at the *end* of a lesson. Why? Ask yourself if you can remember everything in this book so far—well enough to answer questions correctly right now. Compare this with describing how you might read about a single concept within a lesson (like Questions with a Lesson) and immediately answer a question about that concept. When you answer questions immediately, *you forget less while increasing the chances of answering correctly.* Thus, learning improves.

Now, you are going to get a within-lesson question. This experience will be worth more than "big money" to you if you can learn to answer these questions within the lesson because, not only will you learn, but you can also use these same techniques to help your children learn. Please answer the following question. It's important. Don't answer by thinking of the answer, but by either writing the answer in a notebook that you will later use for making summaries or by at least moving your lips to whisper the answer to yourself. Later, you will be shown research that proves how moving your lips when answering increases learning.

Let's start with a very easy question. You can answer this with a single sentence.

Q: Why do questions within a lesson produce more learning than questions at the end of a lesson? (You can look back to find the answer.)

Schemata in Your Brain

Key Feature:

- Schemata is like a mental map that hangs together by association.
- Preexisting schema guides our attention to selective or ignores information.

Schemata have categories. (The category of professional athletics has subcategories of basketball, baseball, and football, and there are still more relations between schemata like skills, younger than 40, and older than 50.) If you are given *key features* of a concept before reading about the concept, you will comprehend the paragraph more effectively than if you have not read the key features. This programming is often called "advanced organizers."

Schemata are like a mental map that hangs together by association. When watching a tennis match, different parts of the match go to different parts of your brain, like the speed of the ball to one area, noise of the crowd to a different area, and the color of the ball to yet another. Scientists tell us that we store information into schemata in our brains. *Schemata have categories and subcategories.* There may be a category of birds with a subcategory of birds of prey or those that swim or fly and so on. The categories are also connected so that information in one category may be linked to a different category, like birds being linked to living things. By using brain imagery, scientists have discovered that *when you are faced with a problem, they can see your brain move into various sections of the brain that contain information that would help find the solution.*

When trying to remember, associate, or understand newly presented information, your brain might look for information in a category such as "hot" and recall "hot potato" or "hot stuff" or even "hot dogs." On the other hand, your brain might move to another category such as "cold" which is *the category of opposites*, such as "up and down," "big and little." The category of cold also has several instances that could be recalled, like "cold feet," "cold hands," and "cold-hearted." Note that these are all body parts, so the brain even has information organized in those subcategories. The brain more or less starts looking for association, moving (connecting) from one category to another as well as looking for information in a category when trying to make associations. (Dreaming is thought to enhance the distribution of memories in different parts of your brain.) Youngsters with limited experiences in life are certainly at a disadvantage for comprehension due to lack of schemata.

Q: How do schemata work?

Parents Can Use the Same Techniques that Effective Teachers Use

Just how are you going to teach critical thinking to your children? Well, since we know what effective teachers do to produce learning in their students, based on achievement tests, compared to ineffective teachers, why shouldn't you use what effective teachers use? You should. Later, you will be told how to utilize a problem-solving coping model of teaching where you show how to problem-solve and correct your errors as you go, but let's start with a more basic approach that is sometimes called *explicit direct instruction* (hereafter called direct instruction) and is based on some simple steps for teaching your students everything from facts to comprehension, as well as problem-solving and critical thinking. Before you use the problem-solving coping method of instruction, you need to get some *basic information* into your students' heads by using direct instruction. You do this by:

- Showing and telling them how to solve the problem.
- Have them show and tell how to solve the problem. (Having them *tell* is very important as they will then be able to process and remember the information more effectively.)
- Give immediate feedback and make corrections.

Q: The three basic steps for teaching are very important so you should try to connect these with a schema (something in your brain.) Simply start by writing the steps. If you do not remember the three direct instruction steps, look above for them, try to remember them, and write, say, or whisper (moving lips) the steps if necessary. You be surprised how well you remember them by doing so.

First, get their attention

Before you can effectively use the basic rules for teaching, you need to get your students' attention . . . and hold it for the entire session. Some people use attention signals to get their pupils' attention. To do this, some teachers say, "Mary, please *pay attention*," or "John, *listen* to me," or "Teresa, *look* at this!" or "This is *going to be on the test*," or even, "*I'm going to show and tell you* how I want you to think about this." Some use silence . . . just stopping until the class gets attentive. And a few shout. All of these may work, but it may drive you crazy if you have to do them time and time again during a teaching session. *Success is one of the most effective ways to keep your youngsters engaged and attentive.* Contingencies, if used correctly, can sometimes be employed to obtain attention and keep it.

It also helps if you are given *key features* of a concept before reading about the concept, as you will comprehend the paragraph more effectively than if you have not read the key features. Again, this programming is often called "advanced organizers."

Basic Rules for Comprehending

Rule 1 Demonstrate reading comprehension

In order to teach your children how to comprehend, *you'll*

need to obtain a match between the material and the information in your students' brains. Then you'll demonstrate, get your students to respond, give feedback, and make corrections if necessary. Listed below are several things *you need to model for them in order for them to comprehend their reading assignments:*

- Model trying to understand every sentence. To start, you can *pause after every sentence or so to think about the sentence.* Demonstrate how you will tell yourself that *you intend to understand every sentence* like, "I'm going to concentrate and keep my attention on every sentence in this section. I must focus. I need to monitor what I'm thinking about and recognize when I'm not concentrating."
- Model how to re-read a sentence when you do not understand. Use the dictionary or electronic device when some words are new or confusing. (Think out loud with such statements as, "I don't get this one. Let me slowly read this again.)
- Model how to *reread the past few sentences* when you do not understand.
- Model how to look ahead for an *example* that will help you understand. ("Well, I've reread the sentence, and I still don't understand. What else can I do . . . I'll look ahead for examples. They always help.")
- Model looking for the definitions and breaking the sentence into parts for analysis, if necessary. You can do this by saying out loud, "Let me think about this. The sentence says that positive reinforcement does not have the same features as negative reinforcement. First, I better find out what is meant by *feature.* Then I better see if I can find the features for positive reinforcement . . . and then I can find the features for negative reinforcement. That way, I might be able to understand the sentence."
- Model how to find help in the dictionary or internet or model how to *ask for help* if you cannot find the meaning of the sentence after doing all the above. Google Home, Amazon Echo and other similar electronic devices can give children definitions of words, how to pronounce words, and even spell them in a second.

Rule 2 Require student responses

Ask your students to demonstrate the understanding of every sentence. You might do this by starting with some selected paragraphs instead of a complete text. That way you can start with something that the youngsters can easily understand and gradually make the assignment more demanding. To determine if they understand a sentence, ask them to paraphrase the sentence—to put it in their own words. *When they come to a sentence they do not understand, prompt them to read the sentence again and use the other strategies.*

Active and passive learning

Learning can best take place when you get your students to *actively* respond. Active responding would be to *say, write, point, compute*, etc. These are things you can see or hear. Passive responses, such as *thinking, visualizing, self-rehearsing*, etc. would *be examples of passive learning,* and unfortunately that's how many students respond in many schools and tutoring situations today. Parents and some teachers may do all the showing and telling as the students passively listen . . . if they are listening at all. Even if they listen, active responding on the part of the pupils is necessary for maximum learning.

Keep in mind that it is important for you to make some kind of overt or covert response when reviewing this chapter if you are to understand and retain the information. According to a study at the *University of Montreal*, students were asked to view a series of words on a screen. One group was asked to think the words (covert practice), a second group asked to move their lips as they thought of the words, and a third group was asked to tell someone the words. Telling the words resulted in the most learning. This is just another piece of evidence showing that you should make some kind of overt response to better remember this chapter.

Example of active learning

Assume that you are teaching punctuation by showing and telling how to put an apostrophe ('s) on the end of a word to show ownership. Using the sentence, *"Larry's book is gone."*

<u>Parent/Teacher</u>: You place an apostrophe before the "s" on the end of the word "Larry" which shows Larry's ownership of the book.

<u>Parent/Teacher</u>: Now you tell why this is done as you show me how to punctuate the word "Bill" so it shows that he owns a bicycle?

<u>Student</u>: I use an apostrophe by putting it after Bill and before adding an "s." (Student does this.)

Rule 3 Give feedback and make corrections

Feedback for comprehension could be such words as "good," "go on," "not exactly there." Corrections could also be prompts like, "You said work was not actually moving something. Now, in this example did someone *try* to move or accomplish something?"

Feedback can range from short feedback like saying "right," to pumps, like "what else?" or correcting misconceptions, providing important ideas, and asking for summaries.

Keep in mind that feedback and corrections with these kinds of questions should help pupils reason and think—to use past information to help answer the questions, to evaluate their answers, and to make coherent summaries that allow the information to be meaningful so the content will be stored into memory.

Reasoning

Reasoning has been found to be an important skill in becoming an intelligent thinker. When participants are taught to use inductive logic, they are able to improve their predictions of real-life events. In this series of chapters, several types of reasoning will be shown, so keep in mind that reasoning cannot be taught in one easy lesson. Parents should continue to seek opportunities for the use of reasoning and teachers should include reasoning in their curriculum.

In this chapter, *criterion reasoning* could be used with the steps for comprehending. *Criterion reasoning* is making a comparison to established criteria. For example, if your children have difficulty with understanding what they are reading have them compare what they have done to the steps for comprehending. They would ask themselves:

- "Did I really try to understand the sentence?" If they answer no, they could then ask themselves,
- "Did I reread the sentence?" They would try to reason whether they had missed a step(s) and how this may have affected their performance. Encourage them to ask themselves how they could find out why they had difficulty understanding the passage. Select several topics with rules or steps for subtraction, division, or grammar, like punctuation and verb tense. You can even use a task, like having them follow the rules for putting together a rocking chair. Have students compare the rules they have completed to what they should have done. The more topics with which you do this, the better your students will understand that they can use reasoning (instead of trial and error) to determine what went wrong.

Parents, Teachers, and Children Together

By working together, parents, teacher, and children can teach and learn the skills to critical thinking much more effectively than they can alone. Parents and teachers: if you are going to be effective in teaching the skills to critical thinking, you must know these steps. How could you demonstrate using the skills if you do not know them? Here are some suggestions that will help you learn the skills yourself while teaching them to your children:

- Use a notebook to record your answers to the questions in each chapter and make notes on such things as the three steps for teaching and the steps for comprehending mentioned in this chapter. You can start now before reading more chapters. You can also find more information on this activity and even a letter to parents about participating at:
http://ed.fnal.gov/trc_new/sciencelines_online/fall97/activity_inserts .html.

- As soon as your children can write, have them write in a notebook the steps for critical thinking, like the steps for comprehending mentioned in this chapter. They can start using the steps for comprehending as soon as they can read proficiently.
- Teachers, you may work with your Parent Teacher Organizations to start a communication program with parents about skills they can teach at home. Copies of the basic rules for teaching or the basic rules for comprehending could be used with examples from this book.

Example of questions at beginning of chapter

Use your own words to answer the questions. You'll learn why in the next chapter

Q1 The steps for basic comprehension are to try to understand every sentence, read the paragraph or sentence again, look up words you do not know, read the paragraph before and after the paragraph you are trying to understand, look for examples and if you still cannot understand, ask for help.

Q2 The basic rules for teaching after getting the children's attention is to first demonstrate by showing and telling, have your students show and tell and them give feedback and make corrections.

Example of questions within a paragraph or section

Before you start to teach comprehension of a subject, make certain your students have the background with the words in the paragraph, they can read the material at an instructional level, and key words should be explained before reading the section.

Q1 Why do questions within a lesson produce more learning than questions at the end of a lesson?

Well, if you have just read something and immediately asked a question about what you read, you will remember it better after reading only a short section than you will at the end of the large section. Since you have increased the likelihood of answering it correctly, you will experience success and success increases the chances that you will answer the question correctly again.

Q2 Schema can be maps with connections of what you have learned or categories for storing information that you have learned. Many experts believe that in order to remember something, you must connect that new information with something you already know. So if you are given the definition or meaning of a key word before reading a section, as you read the section you will have something to connect the new learning with.

Example of Essence

For basic reading comprehension, children should be taught to reread when they do not understand a sentence; if that doesn't work, they should read the preceding paragraph. If still they do not understand, they should look for examples, and if this doesn't help they should look for information on the web or in books. As a last effort, they should ask their teacher or parent for help. The steps for teaching basic comprehension are to get the children's attention, demonstrate how to use the steps for basic comprehension, have the students to use the steps and give them feedback. Just like having students to respond during a lesson, so should parents and teachers as they answer question within a lesson.

Reward Yourself

Questions

As you may recall, you were asked to answer questions presented to you at the beginning of this chapter *when you finished reading the chapter*. Did you do it? You can do it now and then note how well you did this according to a standard:

Questions at the beginning of the chapter

5 points for writing the answers to two of the questions given at the beginning of the chapter.
3 points for moving your lips or whispering the answers to two of the questions at the beginning of the chapter.
1 point for thinking of the answers to two of the questions given to you at the beginning of the chapter.

Questions within the chapter

5 points for answering at least three questions within the lesson by writing the answers in your log book.

3 points for answering at least three questions within the lesson by whispering or moving your lips as you said the answers.

1 point for answering at least three questions within the lesson by thinking of the answers.

Essence

Remember, the essence is the most important part of the chapter, not necessarily a summary. By answering the questions given at the beginning of the chapter, you have probably covered most of the essence and it is not necessary to repeat these. But add whatever else you considered to be most important.

5 points for writing the essence for the chapter.

3 points for saying out loud or whispering the essence.

1 point for thinking of the answer to yourself.

Compare how you performed as compared to a standard:

Outstanding: 13-15 Excellent! You should feel really good about this.

Good: 12 Good; this should give you confidence that you can do this.

Fair: 9 You're hanging in there and have the idea. Now go for the big numbers!

Keep your cumulative record.

Manage your Learning

What you have been asked to do is a form of self-management where you set your own goal, like making at least *Good* on answering the questions at the beginning and within a lesson. Not that someone else sets the goal for you. You also have a plan to get to your goal, like answering questions after reading the chapter, instead of reading a couple of chapters first. And you will determine what kind of reinforcement you will give yourself. It may be just pride for reaching your goal or you may decide to call a friend and talk a little longer than usual. If you follow these steps you will have a better chance of teaching your children these same steps.

Chapter 3
Learning Deeper Comprehension

Do you want your children to be able to figure out the meaning of a reading or a discussion without being told the exact messages? When told some implicit information, don't you want your children to "connect-the-dots" or put things together to figure out the meaning? Sure you do, and that's one of the major features of this chapter. Also, this chapter covers a level of comprehension that is sometimes called "deeper comprehension" because the activities described for retaining information match the manner your children's brains retain information. That happens by organizing information and capturing what you think is conveyed by making a summary or finding the essence. Now you're going to read in more detail how it is done. (You might think that if your children are older, they can already do these things. Perhaps that's true, but most of the research on this has been done with university students and many still don't have all these skills.)

Remember, *key words are words you need to know or learn as you read the chapter.*

Key Words:
Essence
Organizing
Summarizing
Implicit/explicit

Q: Why are inferences important to learning?
Q: Why does organizing and summarizing improve learning?

Parts of Deeper Comprehension

Key Features: *There are three main parts of deeper comprehension:*
• *Inferring* the meaning based on implicit information—information that is not directly stated.

- *Summarizing* what has been presented, noting the essence.
- *Organizing* the material showing the *relationships* among concepts and/or facts.

(Key Features give you something to associate new learning with and provide an organization to what is to follow.) When your students answer factual questions like "who, what, when, and where," they can often find this information in a presentation, but sometimes the information is not there, so they must understand, comprehend, "read-between the lines," or infer what is meant. After they have some implicit and explicit information, they must convert the information to fit their own vocabularies (words) and what they already know so that the material makes sense. That's where summarizing comes in. Finally, if your students can organize the information, noting relations between concepts—like categorizing the information by dates, sequence of events, or how events are related by cause and so on—they will be organizing. Summarizing helps your children make things meaningful, while organizing helps them to record the information so it matches the schemata of their brains.

An inference is the first step

An inference *is reaching a conclusion based on information, (knowledge) and past experience,* even though you may not have read or seen the act you are inferring. It *is something the presenter (like people, books, media) did not necessarily say, do, or write directly. By putting the pieces together, your students can determine the meaning. Make certain the inferring information is valid.*

For example, assume you live near a busy intersection where there have been a number of accidents over the years. Assume that today you hear a loud screeching sound that you infer is from the brakes of a vehicle. Then you hear a crash so loud that it shakes the china in your house. You have a very good idea that an accident happened, even though you did not see it. You put the pieces together based on the sound of tires squealing (that's implicit evidence) and the loud noise (also implicit evidence); however, in this case, you are inferring an accident even though you did not directly view it (*no direct explicit evidence of an accident.*) This is an essential part of critical thinking but not all of it by a long shot.

Inferences can also be a form of inductive logic—finding the patterns or rules that students can predict or use to solve problems. (Inductive logic is a form of logic in which the conclusion is *supported by implicit evidence.)* Assume you have a youngster who has never been taught anything about multiplying; but the student notices a set of multiplied numbers and that as the numbers increase by 10, they always end with a 0, and the first number follows an orderly sequence from 10 to 80. Your student knows how to count from 1 to 10 so he *looks for a pattern or organization* (evidence) that will help him *predict* that the next number in the sequence would be 90. The student does not know for certain that the number will be 90, but based on the pattern, it makes sense to predict a 90. *The basic elements of making an inference are to use information already learned, along with evidence given by the presenter.*

Example of understanding the meaning by an inference

Here's an example of a parent trying to teach her child how to comprehend the meaning of a short story when the meaning was not explicitly stated. This would be an example for preschool children or those in the early grades. The parent wants the child to infer or understand the moral of Aesop's fable, *The Dog and His Shadow.* The last line has been omitted so the child can complete the statement. He must *infer* the meaning.

"A dog was carrying a piece of meat over a bridge above a little stream. As he crossed, he looked down and saw his own shadow in the water. Being a greedy dog and thinking what he saw was another dog with another piece of meat, he wanted both pieces of meat, so he made a snap at the shadow in the water, but as he opened his mouth, the piece of meat he was carrying fell out and dropped into the steam. So the dog lost what he had, and . . . ."

<u>Mom</u>: Richard, what does the story tell you?

<u>Richard</u>: It doesn't always pay to be greedy.

<u>Mom</u>: You've got the idea!

An example for older children

The short story *Death Speaks* was written by William Summerset Maugham. "There was a merchant in Bagdad who sent his servant to market to buy provisions and in a little while the servant came back, white and trembling, and said, 'Master, just now when I was in the market-place I was jostled by a woman in the crowd and when I turned I saw it was Death that jostled me. She looked at me and made a threatening gesture; now, lend me your horse, and I will ride away from this city and avoid my fate. I will go to Samarra and there Death will not find me.' The merchant lent him his horse, and the servant mounted it, and he dug his spurs in its flanks and as fast as the horse could gallop he went. Then the merchant went down to the market-place and he saw me standing in the crowd and he came to me and said, 'Why did you make a threatening gesture to my servant when you saw him this morning?'

'That was not a threatening gesture;' I said, 'it was only a start of surprise. I was astonished to see him in Bagdad, for I had an appointment with him tonight in Samarra.'"

Mom: Millie, what does this story tell you? What's the main idea?
Millie: Oh, it tells me that you can't escape death, no matter how hard you try!
Mom: That's right; but what if you go to the doctor to have him treat what's wrong. Wouldn't that be escaping?
Millie: Oh Mom, that's just extending your time. The grim reaper is going to get us all at the appointed time.

Teaching Children to Make Inferences

There are several activities you can use to help your students get the idea of making inferences. Here a few of them:

- With young children, start by asking them who you are talking about (without mentioning names) by describing the person: Who is this? He goes to our church, has a musical voice, and his eyes open wide when he gets excited.
- Have them describe someone without mentioning their names and let you figure out who they are describing.

- With older children, watch an action DVD or some program with them and pause the program before it ends; then let them figure out how it will end. *Have them list the evidence (from the program and from past experiences).*
- With high school students, have them read a short story and before ending the story, have them infer the outcome. Have them list the evidence for their inference.

Questions for making inferences ("What-if" questions)

Key Features:
- "What if" questions are: "How, Why, What if, and What?"
- How (does this compare, differ)
- Why (did this happen)
- What if (projecting new elements into the information)
- What (will happen, is the point, the essence, the next step)

Again, we're going to use the direct instructional model to teach inferences. To ensure that you and your children capture different levels of comprehension, you should *demonstrate deeper comprehension*, like answering "what if," "how," "what," and "why" questions (hereafter all called "what if" questions.) There may not be specific comments that answer these kinds of questions in your students' reading, so your students must often infer *what* would happen, or *why* it would happen or *how* might it come about. *Inferences use part of what is presented as well as what your children already know*. In all cases you should use the "think-aloud" technique to demonstrate how to use problem-solving and reasoning when you do not know an answer. You need to show and tell how you use deeper comprehension.

Demonstrating how to answer "what if" questions

You should demonstrate how to do "what if" questions to your children in the same way you would with teaching concepts or anything else. You demonstrate by telling children you are thinking of "what if" questions because there is generally no explicit answer in the reading. You must infer the answer to the questions, putting the pieces of the reading or presentation together. Teach the what if questions one at a time using the same reading if possible. Here's an example:

Mom: Next, I could think about a "what if" question, like "What if the sun went out?" Or I could ask myself questions like, "Why does the sun make me warm?" Or I could then explain how the sun makes energy. Let's take the question: "What if the sun went out?" Let me see. . . I know that sun gives us energy in the form of sunlight. I also remember that the sun makes me feel warm when it hits my skin (using something already stored in children's memories) so . . . that's a form of energy . . . so it would get kind of cold, wouldn't it? And plants need energy from the sun as part of photosynthesis, so they can't grow if they don't get it. Wow! That would make a big difference. Let's try another example.

Note: The answer is not in the description presented about the sun but is based on past experience with the sun to formulate an inference.

Summarizing: Finding the essence

The essence is perhaps the most important aspect of what has been presented. It's the heart of the message. Sometimes it's in the message and sometimes your students will need to construct what the essence is based on information that is not presented—just like you do with an inference.

By having your students state the essence in their own words, they will be making *a connection to information already stored in schemata in the gray matter of their brains . . . that's where their own words and experiences are stored.*

Cue yourself to do summaries by writing a note at the end of your assignment or using your smart phone to remind you. Elizabeth Long did a study to determine if summarizing a lesson really makes a difference in learning. She used a cue to remind the students to summarize. And guess what? Those who summarized learned a lot more than those who did not summarize. If you believe this, and really want to understand and retain information presented in this chapter, you might consider using a cue (like a note in your notebook or a sticker on the cover) to make a summary of the material, or maybe even making a chart connecting concepts. (Believe it or not, cues to do or think something really works!)

If you have the general idea of a summary, you should be able to complete the following question:

Q: What is a summary?
(Please write, say, or whisper the answer, because these concepts will be used several times again in future chapters.)

Use information already stored to make meaningful connections

Why does summarizing help with comprehension? It's because when you have your students summarize, you are asking them to connect the "to be learned information," with what they already know (recorded in schema.) If you ask your students to write a paper on what they did during the summer, you will get all kinds of different responses. That's because they are connecting to the different experiences filed in their brains.

You can get a good idea of the experiences of any writer (even me) by looking at the examples individuals use or their description of places and events. That's because they are utilizing information already coded in their gray matter, not something ingenious that they have just materialized. *The bottom line is that you want your students to use their unique schemata of information to make what they are learning more meaningful.*

Organizing
Key Features:
• Organizing is noting the relations between concepts or ideas (may include inferences).
• Organizing can be placing concepts and facts in a hierarchal order.
• Organizing can be finding patterns of connections that match what your students know.

If you really believe information is placed into schema or categories in your youngsters' brains, why not organize the information it so it matches what your children's brains record?

Let's see how to do this. Organizing is also called networking and mapping and is used most often for material of fewer than 1,000 words. It is organizing the major concepts to show how they are related to one another. The relationship might be a part of, type of, leads to, example of, evidence for, or a hierarchical order.

Assume you want to write a paper on the human hand. You could list the parts of bones, knuckles, joints, finger, thumb, fingernails, tissue (epidermis, dermis), leaders, capillaries, blood vessels, and so on. Then you could connect this with the function of the hand (grasp, hold, pull, etc.). For a hierarchical order you could connect this to the arm, trunk, and head. Of course, a well-designed book could do this for you. But if you do your own organizing, it likely will be more effective because you connect new learning to your personal memory bank of experiences.

Abraham Lincoln is one of the best examples of people who learned to organize what new knowledge. Here's how Doris Goodman, in her book *Team of Rivals*, describes Lincoln's organization of what he'd heard: "Unable to sleep, he would reformulate the conversations, until as he recalled, 'Until I had put it into language plain enough, as I thought, for any boy to understand.'" The following day he translated the information and ideas into a language that any of his friends could understand. The key is to organize the material so the learner can understand and remember it. That will produce learning. *So organizing should also contain the major concepts and their relationship to one another.*

Example of using organizing to produce reasoning

Parents and teachers can start to teach organizing at a preschool or first-grade level. Here's an example of a first-grade teacher whom I observed teaching the *concept* of storm and "types of" storms. It made me realize how additional steps might be used to teach reasoning, including the concept of *evidence*. In critical thinking, evidence is an important concept and is necessary in order to establish the validity of a claim or statement.

Here's how reasoning could be used in the teaching of storms:
She *defined* what was meant by a storm (a severe change in the weather).
She told students there were several *types of* storms (thunderstorms, snowstorms, ice storms, dust storms, and even tornadoes).
She then told what *was produced as a result*:
Thunderstorms produce hail, rain, thunder and lightning, etc.
Snow storms produce large amounts of snow.
Dust storms produce dust.
Tornados produce violent winds, severe damage to buildings and trees, and twisted wreckage.
Here's the organization that could have been made with *a couple* types of storms:

Figure 2   Storms and Evidence
                            Storms
                              ↓
                         Types of:
         Thunderstorms   Snow storms

                  Characteristic (Evidence)

Hail, thunder, lightning   High snow, big drifts

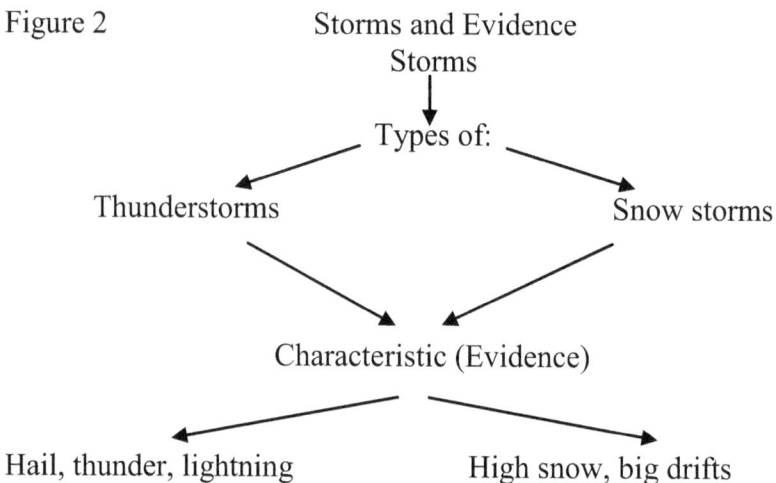

There are different types of storms with different characteristics and evidence. (Evidence is information which tells whether a belief or proposition is true.)

Reasoning from the organizing:
If students have organized this information, they should be able to reason the answer to the following questions:

- If you find dirt and dust all over your car, what kind of storm did you have?
- What kind of evidence would you need to know that there was a snow storm?
- What kind of storm produces thunder and lightning?
- What kind of evidence would you need to believe you had a tornado?

Q: Define what is meant by organizing.

Why Organizing is Important

You certainly need to use some of the techniques for learning described in this chapter before you go to the next chapters. These skills, and those of the succeeding chapters, will prepare your children to acquire *knowledge* that can be used in problem solving, coping, and even critical thinking. Let's look at the value of organizing your learning. According to *Scientific American*, your brain has about one billion neurons. That's about the same memory that you could store on a USB flash drive. Running out of space might be a problem. But your neurons can make about 1,000 connections with other neurons. That increases your memory capacity one million gigabytes. That's enough memory that, if played on a digital recorder, would take 300 years to view. Your brain is organized to make connections to other categories, thus increasing your memory significantly.

Here's another way of looking at the organization of your brain: Assume you have a card in your hand and you want to see if you have the same card in your memory. If your brain did not have connections, you would pretty much need to look at the one million neurons one at a time to make the match. However, since your brain has the neurons organized into categories, you can narrow down your search by selecting categories like birthday cards, gift cards, sympathy cards, graduations cards, and so on. You could even narrow down this group of cards by selecting numbered birthday cards, like first birthday or 40th birthday. You might even reduce this to male or female cards, depending on the specifics of your card and its message. You could do this only if your brain had organized the information in this way. So why not help your brain organize by ordering what you are learning, so your brain connections will be enhanced? If you organized what you have just read in this chapter, you will have created a memory map of the organizing. How do you know that your brain has created a memory map? Well, because you can recall it. If it's not in there, you can't recall it. If you can recall your organization, your brain is ready to fit additional information into your organization—like key concepts.

If you really want to improve your chance of remembering and associating new information to what you have just read, you should take this opportunity to make some organization of some of the major concepts and perhaps enhance them with key features.

Organizing can be unique

In 2016 the *New York Tribune* published an article stating that 97 new locations of mappings of the brain have been found, bringing the total to 180 . . . and more are expected. *But no brain processes scans are absolutely alike.* So your unique background can only associate (connect and remember) information you receive, and it differs from everyone else's. The importance of fitting information into your brain by placing it in your personal schema cannot be overestimated.

Now you already know how we organize information in our brains and those that do it effectively learn more. You should also know by now that you need to associate what you are learning with something you have already learned. Since children learn more if they organize their lessons, why not organize your lesson so they can more effective learn their lessons?

The key features provided in this book are examples of giving your children somewhere that they can file new information. Providing outlines and diagrams will also increase student learning.

Rules for Comprehending

In this chapter the concepts of inferring, summarizing, and organizing were presented as being important to comprehension. The rules for teaching these concepts are the same: modeling, getting students to respond, and providing feedback and corrections.

First you demonstrate how to summarize, organize, and make inferences. Then your students should show and tell how they use what you demonstrated to show and tell how it is done. You give feedback and make corrections and then have them practice. You follow the same rules described in the previous chapter.

Monitor student progress

Now you can monitor the studying of your pupils by looking at their notes and books to determine if your students are summarizing correctly and highlighting the most important aspects of the reading material. You can also *ask questions* about the assignment. If students are doing this correctly, you have achieved a small step in making them independent learners. Next, they should make this a habit.

Teachers, you might consider *having your students make a summary statement of a few sentences after every class they attend,* listing the main ideas and supporting ideas of what was discussed in class. They could do this daily by recording in *a special journal* of summaries. Of course, this could be used for studying for the next exam or a comprehensive exam. It would be a good idea to skim their summaries after a few days and *give them feedback.* After you feel confident they have the skills to make accurate summaries, less monitoring would be required. Parents: you could also look at the summaries to determine what went on in class instead of asking your children what happened during school, and hearing them reply, "Oh, nothing."

Reasoning

Making an inference by using *critical reasoning* is done by studying the definition and trying to use the *information in the definition* to help "reason out" the answer to the question. This is sometimes called *analytical reasoning.* Here's an example:

<u>Dad</u>: Now help me with this next section. (Parents and students do

the next section together, thinking aloud as students write a summary. You can use probes, especially those involving the "what if" questions about environmental biology with your students.)

Dad: Son, your teacher is asking you to answer a question of "why." You have already read about the chemical makeup of the common gasses in our environment, and you know that carbon dioxide is made up of two molecules of oxygen and one of carbon. You've also written a good summary. So now you should be able to answer the question as to *why* people do not realize that there is an increase of carbon dioxide in our air.

Son: I'm not certain, Dad. I guess they don't believe there is an increase.

Dad: That's for sure. They don't believe it, but *why* don't they believe it?

Son: Scientists have been able to measure it, but people don't believe in science.

Dad: That's true for some. Can you think of the composition of the gasses in our environment and see if this would help you?

Son: Well, I'll read the definition in our textbook again. It says carbon dioxide has weight, occupies space, has no shape, and the molecules are too small to be seen . . . that's it! If they can't see it they don't realize it's there!

Dad: People cannot understand that carbon dioxide molecules are so small that they can't see them; consequently, if they don't see their increase it's hard to understand the magnitude of the increase. That's at least part of it! (Son uses evidence from the definition and reasons from there to make an inference.)

Parents, Teachers, and Children Together

Whether you are parent, teacher, or youngster, you play a part in your learning. Here are some things that all of you could do to enhance the chances that all will learn:

- Parents should keep a notebook of answers to the questions along with a summary of what you consider to be important (key concepts) in this chapter.
- Parents should review a youngster's review notebook of what was learned in class each day.
- Teachers should have children daily write the most important things they learned in their notebooks. This might include a summary of the key concepts taught during your lesson or a single concept.
- Children should keep a record of the rules for learning skills like comprehending a reading assignment, writing a summary, and organizing.
- Children should share their notebooks with teachers and parents and use notebooks as study guides.

Essence

Since summaries capture the essence of what has been presented, and they are unique to the individual, *it is more important for your students to make their summaries than for someone else to do them.* It's just like teaching anything: you demonstrate and then get the students to respond. It is now time for you and your students to make personal summary for this and subsequent chapters. You'll use your own words and beliefs to describe what you value most about what was presented and what makes the information more meaningful to you, along with the main ideas and any supporting ideas. (It doesn't have to be long.) This will help you remember the material and even understand it more thoroughly. And don't forget that with a summary (essence) you could make inferences, even though they were not specifically discussed. Try it. Notes and summaries should be precise and concise.

Reward Yourself

Here's how to note how well you did this according to a standard:

Questions at the beginning of the chapter
5 points for *writing* the answers to two of the questions given at the beginning of the chapter.

3 points for *moving your lips* or whispering the answers to two of the questions at the beginning of the chapter.

1 point for *thinking* of the answers to two of the questions given to you at the beginning of the chapter.

Questions within the chapter
5 points for answering at least two questions within the lesson by writing the answer in your log book.

3 points for answering at least two questions within the lesson by whispering or moving your lips as you say the answers.

1 point for answering at least two questions within the lesson by thinking of the answers.

Essence
Remember the essence is the most important parts of the chapter, not necessarily a summary. By answering the questions given at the first of the chapter, you have probably covered most of the essence and it is not necessary to repeat theses. But add whatever else you considered to be most important.

5 points for writing the essence for the chapter.
3 points for saying out loud or whispering the essence.
1 point for thinking of the answer to yourself.

Compare how you performed as compared to a standard:
Outstanding: 13-15 Super; you're in the top group. Give yourself credit.

Good: 12 Nice going! Tell yourself that this is good and to keep it up.

Fair: 9 Keep at it. Tell yourself that you're learning. Now go for the big numbers!

Keep your cumulative record.

Chapter 4
Learning Concrete Concepts

You should know it's difficult to reason without words; well, concepts represent words and your children are going to need to understand the very essence of the concepts they use in order to be able to understand, reason, problem solve, and think critically. There's no getting around it; concepts form the basis for every skill that will be mentioned in this book, so you had better start taking notes as you progress through this chapter. Experts say that concepts are "like the air we breathe." They are "everywhere" and are "essential to our life." Keep in mind that you are not just teaching children how to extrapolate figures or to punctuate a compound possessive sentence; instead, you are teaching them to use the same method you demonstrated to solve all kinds of questions for themselves.

Key Words:
Generalized idea
Concrete concepts
Abstract concepts
Process concepts
Being set

Q: Explain what is meant by a concept and what are the features of a concept?
Q: What are the steps for teaching your children how to learn concepts?

Concepts

Wow! Are concepts ever important! Assume you receive a call from your child's principal. She tells you that your son has broken school rules and they are going to use some negative reinforcement on him. You say to go ahead before you start to think about what your youngster did to break school rules and what she meant by negative reinforcement. Is that a form of punishment? How does it differ from positive reinforcement? If you knew the concept of negative reinforcement, you certainly would have been in a better position to agree or not agree to the consequence . . . and to think critically about the issue. You want your children to learn to be able to discern the difference between all kinds of similar concepts so they can make accurate judgments about problems they will face as they grow older. Defining concepts is an important first step.

Your children learn more concepts than anything else

Teachers teach concepts more than anything else. The school years are filled with the teaching of concepts from kindergarten to high school and on to college. Concepts are the very heart of education. Concepts are represented by words—words that will be used in reasoning, problem solving, comprehension, and critical thinking.

So, what's the definition of a concept? Webster defines a concept as "-- an idea or thought, esp. a *generalized idea of a thing or class of things; abstract notion*." That's not a bad definition. The key is the "generalized idea of a thing or a class of things." A generalized idea means there are instances (examples) of the concept that are alike in some way, and "a class of things" might be such things as the *common features* of birds, like a robin, red bird, sparrow, and hawk. They all belong to the class of birds because they have something in common, like feathers, wings, and they are warm blooded. So birds would be a concept.

Different Types of Concepts

Key Features: There are three major types of concepts:
- Concrete concepts (can touch or see.)
- Abstract concepts (cannot touch or see.)
- Process concepts (have steps.)

Although there are three major types of concepts, this chapter will cover only *concrete* concepts. Abstract and process concepts will be covered in the next chapter. Concrete concepts can be seen and are usually nouns. We'll call these "visible or concrete concepts," like book and tablet. Concepts can also have a hierarchal order ranging from the most encompassing to the very specific. Books could have a category of "types of" that would include large, small, or different colors, like blue and red.

Figure 3   Concrete Concepts

Components

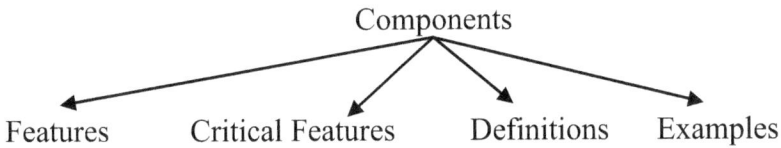

Features   Critical Features   Definitions   Examples

All concrete concepts have features, critical features, definitions, and examples.

Concepts have definitions and critical features
Key Features:
- All concepts have different definitions.
- All concepts have different examples.
- All concepts have critical features that make them different from similar concepts.

In teaching concepts, it is usually most effective to start with a concept definition. This will help your students see the features of a concept like a bird— "they are warm-blooded vertebrates—whose bodies are more or less completely covered with feathers." Some concepts are mental representations of parts of our world, including some things you cannot see or hear but are abstractions of events and situations. Such concepts might be such terms as *engaging*, *explicit*, or *boring*. These are abstract concepts and will be covered in the next chapter. Remember, "*A concept is an idea or thought, esp. a generalized idea of a thing or class of things; abstract notion.*" That's the definition that will be used in this chapter. With concepts your children can start to reason.

Concepts like geometric shapes have features like line and angle, but *concepts also have critical features that make them different from other similar concepts.* Although dogs and cats are domesticated animals, dogs have different features than cats. And bulldogs have different critical features that make them different from collies. All dogs share some attributes in common, like the same number of bones, but the collie has a smaller mouth than a bulldog, longer legs, and a narrower face and longer body.

Q: A reasoning question for your young children: If a tricycle and a bicycle both have wheels, a seat, and you can ride them, what makes a scooter different than a tricycle and bicycle?

Difference between features and critical features
Concepts may have many features, like a "ball" can have many colors, can be large like a beach ball, or small like a golf ball. A ball can *be used* for many things, like playing basketball, soccer, tennis, and golf. Balls can be hit, punched, and thrown. But these are just features; they do not make the critical difference between a ball and a tackling dummy or a sand bag (which can be composed of many colors, be large or small, and can be punched, hit, and thrown.) There are all kinds of examples of balls, like meat balls, cotton bolls, yarn balls, ball bearings. All have color and size (features), but the only critical feature is that they all are rounded or spherical. So we start with a definition of a ball: A ball is a rounded or spherical solid or hollow object.

Concepts have examples

Concepts have examples. All of them do. For example, the concept of square could be a large square, a small one, one painted red, and so on. A concept of men could be Asian men, tall men, bald men, and hairy men. They come in all shapes, sizes, and colors. The same for birds; they come in all kinds of shapes and colors. (The same for bicycles—different colored bikes, mountain bikes, racing bikes, 24-inch wheels, 26-inch wheels and so on.)

Importance of Leaning Critical Features

Assume it is 1935 when 21% of the labor force worked on farms, and you were notified that your great uncle had just died and left his farm to you. You had always lived in the city and don't know a rooster from a hen or a bull from a cow. But you decided it would be an adventure to try farming so you move to the small house with a large barn surrounded with open fields and a stand of timber in the back. A neighbor told you that the first thing you will need is a mule, so you go the cattle auction where all kinds of animals like pigs, turkeys, chickens, horses, and mules are shown and people bid on them. Cattle auctions still exist today.

You had enough money to buy a mule, but the auctioneer talked so fast you had a difficult time understanding him. Then the auctioneer started showing horses, large and small, white and black, and he also started showing mules and donkeys. Mules, horses and donkeys are concrete concepts, but you must know the critical differences or you would go home with a donkey or horse instead of a mule. What exactly do you look for that makes them different? Those are the critical features; and you better hope someone told you what to look for, because if you get a donkey instead of a mule, you'll find how cantankerous the creature can be when you connect him to a plow. Here are the features to look for:

Look at the mane	Appearance and size	Sound
Horse: long, thick mane	Larger than donkeys	Neighs
Mule: thinner mane	Head larger than horse	Heehaws
Donkey: mane sticks up	Smaller than horse and mule	Brays

Tail: donkey has tail like cow with bunched hair at the end, horse has thick tail,
Heads: Donkeys and mules have heads that are larger in proportion to bodies, than do horses.

That's a great number of features! What are the critical features that make them different every time, with every example? Many times the definition will tell you . . . but not always. Here's what the online dictionary says about the three animals:

Horse: a solid footed domesticated mammal, with a flowing mane and tail, used for riding, racing, and carrying and pulling heavy loads.
Mule: offspring of donkey and horse, used as a beast of burden

Donkey: a domesticated hoofed mammal, of the horse family, with long ears and a braying call, used as a beast of burden.

Let's face it: definitions *do not always* tell you the critical features. Most the time they might, but you need to depend on it when you trying to tell a cancer cell from a normal cell. If you examine the features listed above the definitions, you can always tell the difference by the sounds they make—always. That's a critical feature. Also donkeys have larger ears—always. This is a critical feature. Horses have a thicker tail than donkeys whose tails are like a cow—always; you can depend on it. And the size of the head, in proportion to the body, is larger than that of a horse—that's always the case. Mules make a different sound than horses. Every time, with no exceptions!

If you can teach children to find the critical features, you will have taught them a great deal more than the concepts listed in their books. By learning this skill, they will realize that they must search for critical features using the steps or rules to better learn these differences. Have your students make a table, just as was done above, and then reason by comparison which attributes are critical for the concepts.

Teaching Concrete Concepts

You should use the basic steps for direct instruction to teach concrete concepts by showing and telling, by having your students show and tell how to work the problems or answering the questions, and by giving feedback and make corrections if necessary.

You could build a *concept descriptor* to help them see the difference between the concepts like the one below:

	Carries people/	Goes straight up and down/	Carries cargo
Elevator	Y	Y	Y
Escalator	Y	N	N

After showing and telling how to get the correct answer, *have your students tell how to obtain the correct answer and explain why their answer is correct.* (You are requiring an overt response, and remember that overt responding produces more learning.) If they have trouble remembering what you said, you can guide the youngsters by telling them how to do the problem again as they work it. However, before your lesson is finished, make certain that your students can show and tell how to get the answer without guidance.

Do not give your students practice questions to do by themselves until they can show and tell how to answer the problem. Having students *verbalize the critical features* is the step that most tutors miss. It's an overt response and makes learning more complete. After they can repeat how to solve the problem you demonstrated, they then need to practice. Here's how your students should respond after Mom has demonstrated how to identify the critical features of an elevator and an escalator:

<u>Mom</u>: Now you tell me the critical features of each.
<u>Student</u>: Well, the elevator goes straight up and down and the escalator goes up at an angle, like stairs. The elevator can carry merchandise as well as people and the escalator just carries people.
<u>Mom</u>: Fine.

Q: Explain what your students must do before being given practice on the concept just taught.

The most basic way to make corrections is to have your students:
• Look at or read the question again while you give students five seconds or more seconds to respond. Another way is to say "Oops," look at the problem again.
• If the students cannot answer the question, repeat the demonstration, ask students to show and tell as they complete the problem, give them feedback, and make corrections again using different words and different examples.

But there are also ways to help your students figure out the answer to the question. Using probes such as "What else?" or questions like, "What does the term mean?" or the parent or teacher could ask for a contrast like, "If this is as you say, what the other would be?" Hints like, "It starts with the letter *A*" should be discouraged as that may actually lower performance.

Concrete Concepts Are Essential to Reasoning

If you think concrete concepts are so basic and that elementary school and older children already know most of them, you better think again. Children may be able to consistently point out how dogs and cats are different or how triangles differ from rectangles. They may be able to correctly point out that concepts are different, but they *may not be able to verbalize how the concepts differ in critical features*, and it is the critical features that are essential to reasoning.

Example of reasoning planets from asteroids

Here's an example of reasoning planets from asteroids: First, have your children look up the definition of a planet. The definition should include the critical features. There are three of them:

1. Orbit the sun
2. Large enough that gravity causes them to form a ball
3. Gravity strong enough to pull and sling objects off into space and out of their orbit.

(Knowing this should help your children to reason why comets and asteroids are not planets.) Asteroids larger than 100 km are usually round. Some asteroids have moons; and so do some planets. Mercury is our smallest planet with a diameter of 4,879km, and Jupiter is the largest. Pluto is 2,372km. Have your students list the common features and critical features, like in the example below:

Planets
Round if over 100km
Larger than 4,879km
Slings objects out of their orbit

Asteroids
Not round if less than 100km
Smaller than 4,879 km
Have object in their orbit

Now that your students know the critical features of planets in our solar system, they should be able to reason the answer the following questions:

Q: What makes a planet different from an asteroid?
Q: Name two ways planets and asteroids are alike.
Q: Since Pluto is smaller than 4,979km, is it a planet or an asteroid *by our definition*?
Q: If Jupiter is the largest planet, is it larger than Earth?
Q: Could there also be other objects that orbit the sun that are planets or asteroids? (Yes)
Q: If your definitions and information on planets and asteroids are correct, would you say that there could also be additional critical features between the two?

Help your children reason from the critical features of a planet that make them different from asteroids.
- Since a planet must be 4,879km in size
- Since Pluto is less than 4,879km,
- Therefore, it is not a planet. (Actually it is called a minor planet.)

The above example could help you develop similar reasoning questions on any number of concepts like books and newspapers, trucks and trains, and so on. Once your children have learned the importance of finding the critical features of a concept, they should not only be able to tell how they differ from similar concepts, they should also be able to answer a variety of questions like those in the above example. This is called set-based reasoning, based on category or membership.

Being Set to Look for Critical Features

It's more important for your children to learn to look for critical feature of concepts than learn single concepts like planets and asteroids. Teachers, this question is for you and it's important: When you ask your children to look up definitions of concepts and have them look for the features, have you ever told your students that one concept is different *from all other concepts* and a feature may be called a *critical* feature? If children knew this, and understood it, they would be able to use reasoning to compare the critical features of such concepts as mitosis and meiosis. They could find out for themselves what make the difference, because they have learned a "set" to look for critical features among concepts. A set means a predisposition to look for certain things and it can be taught and learned through practice.

Teaching children to be "set" to look for critical features of concepts should be required in every school curriculum. Don't make them discover this, tell them. Have children look for critical features enough, and it will become a habit. Keep in mind the questions at the beginning of each chapter are designed to make you set to look for the answers as you read the chapter.

Parents, Teachers, and Students Together

• Teachers, your lessons are filled with concepts, many of which have similar concepts that can be distinguished by pointing out the critical features of each. Do it with a lesson when the occasion arises. Teach your children to be on the lookout (set) for critical features when discussing concepts.
• Students copy the definition of critical features and have an example in your notebook for reference.
• Parents, take the time to point out how concepts differ. With young children point out how objects around the house and garage are *alike* and *different*. With older children you could point out the critical features of different airplanes, cars, and equipment.

Essence

As you determine the essence, keep in mind that what you generate as the essence should not be regurgitating what you have read in this book. Rather, it should be in your own conception in your own words. That way it will be remembered more easily.

Reward Yourself

Here' how to note how well you did this according to a standard:

Questions at the beginning of the chapter
5 points for writing the answers to two of the questions given at the beginning of the chapter.
3 points for moving your lips or whispering the answers to two of the questions at the beginning of the chapter.
1 point for thinking of the answers to two of the questions given to you at the beginning of the chapter.

Questions within the chapter
5 points for answering at least three questions within the lesson by writing the answer in your log book.
3 points for answering at least three questions within the lesson by whispering or moving your lips as you said the answers.
1 point for answering at least three questions within the lesson by thinking of the answers.

Essence
Be certain to write your summary or essence and keep it in your log for later use. Remember the essence is the most important parts of the chapter, not necessarily a summary. By answering the questions given at the first of the chapter, you have probably covered most of the essence, and it is not necessary to repeat these. But add whatever else you considered to be most important.
5 points for writing the essence for the chapter.
3 points for saying out loud or whispering the essence.
1 point for thinking of the answer to yourself.

Compare how you performed as compared to a standard:
Outstanding: 13-15 Outstanding! Say nice things to yourself, like "I did it!"
Good: 12 You're doing well! Tell yourself that you are proud of

yourself.

Fair: 9 Your performance says you are likely to learn a lot. Try for the next level.

Keep your cumulative record.

Chapter 5
Learning Abstract and Process Concepts

Parents have a wonderful opportunity to teach abstract concepts because children hear and see abstract concepts occurring at home as much as at school. Abstract concepts exist as thoughts or ideas and have no physical or concrete existence. In other words: you cannot see or hear them as you can with concrete concepts. Because you can't see or hear them, you teach them through examples until your children "get" the idea. Here's where parents come in: you and your children see examples of abstract concepts every day at home, eating out, as you go on a trip, as you read, as you watch a movie or television, and even as your children work and play together. All you have to do is point them out and give them a name. Teachers need to be on the alert to point out and name abstract concepts when they see examples of them. And don't forget, you are teaching children to learn how to deal with abstract concepts with any school subject, from geography to calculus as well as to deal with words that offer real-life challenges.

Key Words:
process concepts
abstract concepts
positive and negative reinforcement

Q: What are abstract concepts, and why are they necessary for reasoning?
Q: What is the difference between an abstract concept and a process concept?

Abstract Concepts

A great deal of your children's reasoning and critical thinking is done with abstract and process concepts. They can't see these concepts, like they can with *concrete concepts*, so you must help them figure out the idea as to what the features and critical features are. With *process concepts*, children need to follow steps, like the steps for multiplying and dividing.

Abstract concepts are just in your mind. You can't see the abstract concept of "tie," but you can see or hear someone give you an example of tie, like in tying your shoes, or tying a rope to a boat. And it's easier to teach the concept of tie by showing, rather than telling how to tie shoes.

Figure 4   Similarities and Differences among Concepts

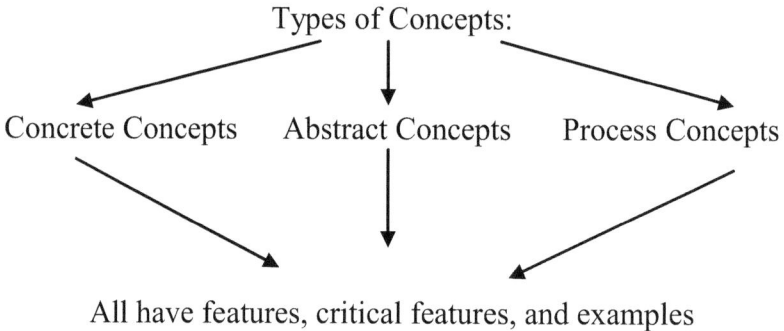

Types of Concepts:

Concrete Concepts   Abstract Concepts   Process Concepts

All have features, critical features, and examples

A quick review of concepts
- All concepts have different definitions.
- All concepts have different examples.
- All concepts have critical features that make them different from similar concepts.
- Some concepts have steps.
(Facts have no definitions or examples.)

Abstract concepts have definitions, but most of the time they are filled with abstract concepts themselves. For example, *"justice" is defined as a just action or treatment.* So "just action" is an abstract concept that also needs to be defined. Therefore, you must use several examples to help your children understand the meaning of the concept. For example, for the concept of "ironic," you could *show a picture* of people going into a health club by using an escalator instead of the stairs, or you could tell about an obese man telling people how to lose weight. Pictures and drawings help children understand the meaning of abstract concepts. Although examples are probably the most effective way to teach abstract concepts, you still need to point out the definitions and critical features, if you can.

Example of teaching an abstract concept by examples

Abstract concepts are sometime difficult to explain. Can you explain "concentricity" or even the color "pink?" You must use several examples to teach these concepts. *Listen to Mom as she teaches her student the concepts of fast, slow, and "compared to:"*

Mom: Giving definitions: When we say people are slow, we mean people take their time and are not in a hurry. When we say people are fast, we mean they are quick and speedy. When we say, "compared to," we mean noting similarities and differences. Let me give you some examples:

Mom: Here's a picture of a rabbit and a turtle. The rabbit can run fast, compared to the turtle who runs slow—if he runs at all.

Mom: Here's a picture of a car and a scooter. The car goes fast, compared to the scooter that is slow.

Mom: Here's a picture an airplane and a man running; the airplane goes fast compared to the man running.

Mom: Now you tell me what is meant by slow and fast and "compared to," and give me an example of something fast compared to something slow.

Child: Fast means to do something rapidly, and slow means to take your time in doing something. "Compared to," means to compare (or measure) one to another on some skill or difference. You talk fast; I talk slow . . . compared to you . . . but Uncle Bill talks slower than any of us. That's an example.

Mom: *You* did it! Doing that so quickly should make you proud!

Some abstract concepts have critical features

Although abstract concepts may be difficult to define, the critical features can sometimes be specified clearly like in the following example. (This is an example that many college students have difficulty with.) Example: What's the critical feature of positive reinforcement that makes it different from negative reinforcement?

Let's start with a definition of positive reinforcement: positive reinforcement is a stimulus (something) given after the *desirable behavior* (like making 100 on a test for the first time), that increases the chances the *desired behavior* will occur again. If a student earns a score of 100 on a test for the first time (desired behavior) and you immediately take him to the corner ice-cream shop to eat chocolate ice-cream (stimulus), it will be a positive reinforcement *only if it increases the behavior* (he makes a 100 again the next time). So, positive reinforcement can be called positive reinforcement *only if it increases* the chances (probability) that the behavior will occur again. It's after the fact . . . you don't call it reinforcement until it increases the behavior . . . and the stimulus event can be almost anything.

Here are some examples of stimulus events that may (not for sure) increase the behavior of drinking orange juice: Saying, "Nice going," or "Neat! Have some chocolate." But what about saying "Go stand in the corner," or whispering, "You look awful?" Believe it or not, all could increase the behavior of some children, although it is not highly likely. Any one of these events could increase the drinking of orange juice, but we'll never call any of them reinforcement *unless they actually do increase* the drinking of orange juice. (Yes, reprimands have been known to increase tantrum behavior in some children! That's reinforcement.) You don't call a volcano eruption and eruption until it erupts. So don't call a reward or treat or reprimand reinforcing until it increases the behavior that it followed. Take a look at the features and critical features in these two similar concepts:

Positive Reinforcement	Negative Reinforcement
Desirable behavior occurs	Desirable behavior occurs
Something given after the behavior	Something *taken away after* the behavior
Increases the behavior	Increases the behavior

Notice that all the features are the same except that in positive reinforcement, the stimulus (the something) *is given after* the behavior, and in negative reinforcement the stimulus (the something) *is taken away* after the behavior (like you removed the painful gravel in your shoe and it reduced the pain, making it more likely that you will remove the gravel again when you feel pain from a gravel.) The critical feature for positive and negative reinforcement is something is *given* (or happens) after the behavior; and for negative reinforcement, something is *removed* after the desired behavior. Notice that all the features are the same except that in positive reinforcement, the stimulus (the something) *is given* after the behavior and in negative reinforcement the stimulus (the something) *is taken away.*

Example of positive reinforcement:
The teacher starts to *praise* (adding something) *after* the child a good test score (behavior) and the youngster's scores *increase.*
The teacher *gives* a child a paper clip for every problem worked accurately and he increases the accuracy of his work.

Example of negative reinforcement:
You removed the painful glove (*takes away* pain) from your hand and it reduced the pain making it more likely that you will remove the glove again if you feel pain. Your child eats his spinach (behaves) and you let him leave the table (*removes or takes away* sitting there so he can go play). If this *increases* the changes of his eating his spinach, it would be called negative reinforcement.

Q: What are the major characteristics of abstract concepts?

Process Concepts

Process concepts are also abstract concepts with some steps or rules. Take for example the mathematical concept of *dividing. You start with a definition* of "separate into parts." (Notice the word "separate" is also an abstract term.) When your students have mastered this concept, then you are able to *teach them the steps (process)* for solving mathematical problems.

Example of how to teach a process concept using rules or steps

<u>Mom:</u> You're going to learn something new today so listen carefully. You're going to learn about fractions. A fraction is "a numerical quality that is not a whole number" (gives examples). Look at these pictures. (Mom continues on until her students comprehend the meaning of a fraction.)

<u>Mom:</u> *I'm going to show you the steps* for adding fractions now that you know how to reduce fractions as a start. *Watch me* with this first problem. I'm going to follow several steps to solve this problem of adding fractions.

I'm going to add the following: $1/8 + 6/8 =$?

Step 1 Make certain the fractions have the same denominator—and they do. It is 8.

Step 2 When you add, you keep the denominator the same /8.

Step 3 Add the numerators together $1 + 6 = 7$

Answer: $1/8 + 6/8 = 7/8$

Q: What's an example of an abstract concept not mentioned before in this book?

Teaching Abstract and Process Concepts

You teach abstract concepts in the same manner you teach concrete concepts: you show and tell *using a great number of examples.* Identify the critical feature just as was done in the example of reinforcement. Since you want children to grasp the idea of concepts, you can show figures, charts, pictures, and even movies to help them gain understanding. Stories, books, and newspaper articles can teach honor, courage, loyalty, insight, daring, and compassion. All are abstract concepts and are difficult to define. (Facts are taught differently than concepts and will be covered in the next chapter.)

Example of process concepts

Since process concepts are abstract concepts, you should first teach your children the abstract concept, like what the sum or fraction is or what is meant to tie something—like their shoe strings as described above. Then you can teach the steps or process to obtain an answer. For example, after getting the idea of what is meant by "tie," youngsters must follow some steps to actually tie their shoes even though they may know what the word means. Here's how to start the process of tying your shoes:

Mom: I'm going to show and tell you how to tie your shoes. The first thing you do in tying your shoe is to hold one string in each of your hands (demonstrates and student responds).
The next step would be to cross the strings (demonstrates and student responds).
The next step would be to place one under the other (demonstrates and student responds).
Then you pull tight against your shoe and so on (demonstrate and student responds).
Then have your children to continue to say the steps as they do them. (Continue steps).
Finally, you give feedback and corrections, if necessary.

Q: What is the most basic method for teaching abstract concepts?

Discriminative corrections

When your children make a mistake, you want them to correct the mistake by themselves, if they can. By self-correcting they will learn a method to find the answer when you are not around to help them. You want them to self-monitor their thinking by asking themselves such questions as: "Does my answer make sense?" "Did I do something wrong?" "Did I miss a step?" "Did I misread the question?" This is a very important part of critical thinking—to monitor one's thinking, evaluate it before making a conclusion, and ask oneself if the conclusion makes sense.

First ask your students to read, look, or listen to the problem again. After they have focused their attention on the problem, you can demonstrate other ways to evaluate their answers. One method to get your students involved in self-correcting is called the *discriminative* method. This method requires your students to do more reasoning.

Discriminative corrections is giving feedback on the correctness of an answer and then providing additional information at the same time. The information presented is the correct answer, usually the definition, steps, or examples. If your students have a written answer or have selected a multiple-choice answer, they can then compare their answer with the definition (or an example). This may be enough for your students to see an error and be able to make the correct response in the future. You may also provide a lecture with the discriminative correction method. In this book, this is the method that will be referred to most often. Later chapters will expand on this method and show the steps for using problem solving/coping or discovery learning. Here's an example:

Teacher: No, that's not right. Look at the problem again. The mode is the number *that occurs most often* (definition), not the average as you have indicated. In this series of numbers 22, 09, 14, 12, 14, and 07, 14 would be the mode because it occurs twice and no other number occurs more than that. Now you compare what I just showed you with what you did on the problem you missed. Do this one as you tell me how to do it and *why*.

Example of making corrections

Parents don't need to wait to look at school work or give a test before teaching concepts to their children. You can begin before your children ever start school. Here's an example of Mom teaching Sarah to identify a critical feature of an abstract concept as they are doing pleasure reading:

Sarah reads: "The fox asked, 'Is your voice as sweet as your form is beautiful?' The crow was so happy in his praise that she opened her mouth."
Mom: Sarah, what is meant by praise?
Sarah: Saying something nice. (Not a clear definition)

Mom: Think about that for a moment. (Pause) If I say, "I like you," I'm being nice; but is it praise?

Sarah: No . . . I'm not certain.

Mom: Let me tell you what praise is: Praise is *approval*. Like if I said, "You did a good job cleaning up your room today." That would be *approval*. If I said, "I'm so proud of you for helping me do the laundry," that would be *admiration*. I *admire* you for doing such things as the laundry. So you can see from these *examples*, there's a difference between saying, "I like you" and *praise for something you have done*. You must do something before you are praised or admired. Now tell me in your own words what praise is and give me an example?

Sarah: Well . . . praise is telling someone you liked what *they did*. For example, if I clean up my room and you like it, you tell me I did a good job.

Q: How do you teach abstract concepts?

Q: What are the differences between abstract concepts and process concepts?

Q: What are the basic steps for correcting?

Reasoning

Abstract concepts are used to reason all the time. For example, when marrying, the person, priest, minister, or rabbi marrying you will possibly use the words, "—to love and to cherish from this day forward until death do you part." Let's examine the word "cherish." Let's see what your obligation is and use this in reasoning when you marry. First, start with a definition from the *Free Dictionary*: Cherish means to "protect and care for someone lovingly." Most of you have seen many examples of cherish so you know what it means. However, your children may not know so let's take some examples of cherish from the *Blog Life*:

Telling people how you feel about them that is positive,
Saying grateful things,
Showing your love,
Send messages of love,

Make someone feel of value.

Here's a scenario where the abstract concept of "cherish" is important in answering the question as to whether Franklin's wife cherishes him:

Franklin goes to court to ask for a divorce from Hillary. He says his wife has broken her wedding vows because she does not cherish him even though she made this vow. She never smiles at him, doesn't talk to him unless asked a question, shows no affection, almost never touches or caresses him, and sleeps in another bedroom. She doesn't help with the laundry or house chores. When he asks her a question, she seems annoyed. She's just not friendly! Franklin works a 40-hour week and spends the weekends cleaning the yard and house. Hillary refuses to go to dinner with him or a movie . . . she won't even exercise with him. She stays on the phone all day talking to her five sisters and her mother. When he comes home, she is on the phone and motions to him to be quiet by waving her hand without looking at his face . . . no smiles.

Hillary says she loves Franklin. She just can't show it. She says she cooks some of the time, but he doesn't like cabbage, spinach, broccoli, liver, tongue, or Rocky Mountain oysters. She doesn't like for him to touch her because it makes her skin creep. She can't help it. She doesn't like to talk to him because she has nothing to say. She loves her sisters and mother and must talk to them. They need her attention. He doesn't seem to mind doing the housework. She doesn't want a divorce.

You can use two types of reasoning here. One is analytical: breaking the problem into parts and evaluating each part. That is noting that the definition of cherish has parts given in the examples (protect, care, lovingly). You need to define *protect* (keep safe from harm or injury) *care* (provide what is necessary for health, protection, and welfare) and lovingly (with love and care). The second type of this reasoning is matching the definition (parts) and examples (evidence) to Hillary's behavior that demonstrates that Hillary shows no cherishing behavior. For example, was there any evidence that she said *grateful things,* or *made him feel valued?* You should see that there is little evidence that Hillary protects, cares, or does things lovingly if you match her behavior with the examples and definition.

Essence
You know the importance of organizing and summaries, so don't forget to help your brain to organize and remember by summarizing the steps for teaching abstract and process concepts.

Reward Yourself

Here's how to note how well you answered the questions according to a standard:

Questions at the beginning of the chapter
5 points for writing the answers to two of the questions given at the beginning of the chapter.
3 points for moving your lips or whispering the answers to two of the questions at the beginning of the chapter.
1 point for thinking of the answers to two of the questions given to you at the beginning of the chapter.

Questions within the chapter
5 points for answering at least three questions within the lesson by writing the answer in your log book.
3 points for answering at least three questions within the lesson by whispering or moving your lips as you said the answers.
1 point for answering at least three questions within the lesson by thinking of the answers.

Essence
Remember the essence is the most important parts of the chapter, not necessarily a summary. By answering the questions given at the first of the chapter, you have probably covered most of the essence and it is not necessary to repeat theses. But add whatever else you considered to be most important.

5 points for writing the essence for the chapter.

3 points for saying out loud or whispering the essence.
1 point for thinking of the answer to yourself.

Compare how you performed as compared to a standard:

Outstanding: 13-15 You certainly deserve being bragged on. Tell yourself you're dedicated to learning to be a super teacher of critical thinking.

Good: 12 This is good work. It's equivalent to a B in some college courses. Tell yourself that you are learning and are going to be able to help children learn critical thinking.

Fair: 9 You're learning and it will show up on the test. Try for the next level.

Keep your cumulative record.

Chapter 6
Learning Facts

Many people think that learning of facts is just to practice rote memory . . . say it again, again, and again. Well that works, but there are more effective ways to learn facts. For example, you can reduce what you want your students to learn into parts, like paragraphs or sections of the Gettysburg Address. Then after the first part is mastered, teach the second, and then put the first part with the second, and practice, then add a third part, and so on. You can also use mnemonics (something that helps children remember) like making a word out the first letter of what is to be remembered or associate it with something you already know, like a person who has a similar name. And it may surprise you to know that facts can be used in reasoning. Facts are important!

Key Words:
Facts
Who, what, when, where
Baseline
Mnemonics

Q: Explain how your brain processes facts differently from concepts.
Q: What is meant by "over-loading your brain?" And why is this important?

Facts Are Important

Facts are important. You've heard parents say, "Teachers don't need to teach all those facts and have children just memorizing the answers!" Well, that's what you do *when you teach facts; you get the children to memorize the facts (questions and answers).* And don't think facts aren't important! Facts are supposed to be indisputable. If that's correct, wouldn't that assist your children in doing reasoning and critical thinking? Don't you think it's a good idea for children to know their names? or their addresses? or date of birth? or the name of the president? or the number of pi carried out to two decimals

(1.61)? These are all facts. And don't think they aren't important to critical thinking. Wouldn't you hate to have a chemist who didn't know the danger of nitric acid making decisions for you?

The teaching of facts is much like the teaching of concepts, except that you cannot explain how to get the answer. It's just memorizing. When teaching a math concept like borrowing, you can explain how to do the borrowing. But with facts, like the states and their capitals, you cannot explain that the capital of Tennessee is Nashville. It just is the capital. There's nothing to explain. You simply tell the student the state and capital. Also, *in learning facts, your students must practice, practice, and practice* . . . and use mnemonics in order to remember the facts. With concepts, the learner needs only to get the idea in order to answer questions about concepts.

Of course, as children become older many of them have already developed ways to identify and remember facts by using mnemonics techniques. If you believe your students have already mastered these skills, check them out just in case, so you can give them some pointers.

Figure 5   How Your Brain Works with Facts

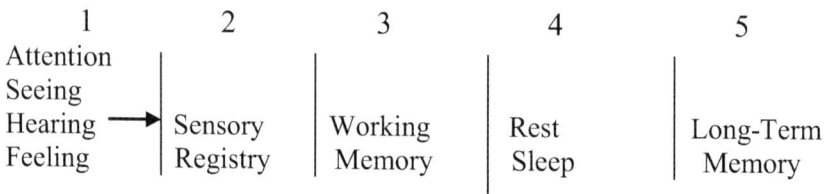

1	2	3	4	5
Attention Seeing Hearing → Feeling	Sensory Registry	Working Memory	Rest Sleep	Long-Term Memory

In order to remember facts, you must see or hear the message through your senses. You then repeat it until you can make the information meaningful by associating it with something you already know. Rest and sleep then help you transfer the information into long-term memory.

Your brain works hard to remember facts

The rules you will receive in this chapter are consistent with how children process information. Processing information means how we remember and recall. There are four features to processing information. Here's a simplified version of how this takes place:

Make certain your students see or hear the facts

It's a fact that *your brain acts differently in learning facts than in learning concepts.* Here's what happens when you learn facts: First, *the information must register on your students' senses (called sensory register)*—they need to see or hear (or feel) what you are presenting. This step is also true for concepts. That's why tutors say such things as, "Now listen to this!" Such statements attempt to make certain that the students hear the tutor and the words go to their brains.

Rehearse the message

Once your children hear the message, if it contains unfamiliar facts, your students must rehearse them until they can transform the message in order to remember it—*and on average they can only handle about seven pieces of information at this stage, and this lasts only a few seconds. This rehearsing is called working memory.* With facts, one of the reasons for the rehearsal is because the neurons from the sensory register fire rapidly. It's like hitting a piano key. It makes a sound for just a second no matter how long you hold it down. So your students don't have a long time to process it without rehearsing it. If you give your students another fact while they are trying to rehearse the first one and then a third one, you likely will wipe out the first and second one (maybe the third one, too) before any learning can take place.

With strings (several words) of concepts, your students have a little more time to remember the information . . . about a minute unless they make it meaningful or continue to rehearse. Haven't you thought to yourself that you better check the oven to see if the roast has cooked; and when you get to the kitchen, you say to yourself, "Why am I here?"

Make the learning meaningful

This step is *making the material meaningful,* and it may take some work and time. Your students might chunk (or reduce) the information, so instead of having to remember 732432198799, the learner might reduce this to 732, 432, 198, 779 (four units instead of nine numbers). Or the learner might put a decimal point in to make it sound more like money, i.e. $7.32, $4.32, $1.98, $7.79. Yet the learner might associate this with items in his room, like a shirt cost $7.32 and a belt to go with the shirt, that cost $4.32 and the 32 really helps here because the learner makes a connection that the items end in the same amount. By associating the cost with items in the room, the two will be connected and the learning improved.

If your students are trying to remember some written Chinese words, they will start searching in their memory banks for anything that might help them remember the Chinese words. An English word that *sounds similar* would help . . . maybe a combination of two English words. And what does the lettering remind them of? What is it similar to? A picture, words, or whatever? Can they reduce it into parts and make an association with each part representing something they already know?

If there's a great deal of information presented, like in the above examples, you may be in deep trouble since you can only handle about seven items at one time (like seven nonsense words). That's just one reason the facts should be presented in *small groups* and practiced before being presented again.

Rest and sleep

After studying, getting rest or sleep seems to be beneficial to problem solving and to the recall of concepts. *But facts can quickly fade away without practice*, usually because other learning interferes with what has been learned. There's more on this in the chapter on problem-solving. (Children who sleep more make better grades. See this study in the Critical Thinking chapter.)

Make structure out of chaos

Although making structure out of chaos is not a form of reasoning or critical thinking, your students will learn that they can organize information so it can be remembered. This will add to their knowledge and make them more effective critical thinkers.

Q: What are some steps for teaching facts?

Mnemonics

A mnemonic is anything that can be used as an aid for memorizing information. It's a form of making things meaningful. Patterns consist of letters or words, images, rhymes, positions; even numbers can help us remember. In time, facts can become connected to each other and to other things already in your brain.

So one of the ways to remember a fact is to use what you already have stored in your head to help to connect with new facts. Since you already know what knuckles are, and they have a top and space between them, you can use these *concepts* to help learn such facts as which months have 30 and which have 31 days. You start with the *top of the first knuckle* as the first month, January. You call that 31. Go in *between* the next knuckle and call it 30 days. You continue going top to between the top and in between until you get to the top of the little finger knuckle, count it again and go back; doing the same thing as you name the months. This applies to every month except February.

Another technique often heard on television and radio every spring and fall is how to remember to change your clocks from daylight savings time to regular and vice-versa. Since you already know the concepts of spring and fall, you use it to guide you in setting your clock back or forward with the following saying:

Spring: clocks *spring* forward
Fall: clocks *fall* backward

When I was in the early grades, we were told to know the year Columbus discovered America. That's something every kid is expected to know. As I walked home that evening from school, an older boy told me a little rhyme that would work:

In 1492,
Columbus sailed the oceans blue;
He hit a bump and skinned his rump,
And made it black and blue!

Q: Why do mnemonics make learning of facts more effective?

Rules for Teaching Facts

The basic rules for tutoring facts are much the same as for teaching concepts and making corrections, only you should present them in a somewhat different manner. You show and tell by presenting the question and the answer. Here's an example:

Show and tell the question and answer
Ask the question and tell the answer. You can say: 'I'm going to teach you the states and their capitals. Let's start with Tennessee. Tennessee is a state and the capital of Tennessee is Nashville."

Have student tell the question and answer
Make certain you have your children connect the question (stimulus) with the answer (response). Have the student say the question and answer, like this:
Teacher: "Now you tell me the capital of Tennessee."
Student: "The capital of Tennessee is Nashville" (not just Nashville).

Provide feedback with positive consequences
Key feature:
• Consequences, like praise or tangible rewards that occur after your youngsters' behaviors, if perceived as positive, may increase the behaviors. There are called positive consequences. The focus in this book will be on the positive consequences.
• Success and social are some of the most effective consequences.

Success
Success is one of the best motivators around, and it will improve student attention. As you know, what *you believe to be success may not be the same to your youngster.* Success can come from some simple things such as adjusting the curriculum so students can answer most of the questions. And does it ever increase motivation! Youngsters who are not attentive and do not do their

lessons suddenly become interested and work diligently on their lessons when they can solve the problems.

Success can drive your brain

Wow! Can success ever change your behavior! We already know success can stimulate the pleasure areas of your brain. But other things happen, too: It can change the chemical composition of your bloodstream as well as altering the chemistry of your brain to give you an opportunity to process information. Scientists have long known that animals that win a battle for dominance, a female, territory, or a herd are emboldened by their wins, making them more likely to win the next battle. It also happens to the football players, basketball players, and even chess players. They become more likely to win the next home game because they expect to win. Tennis players who win the first match have a 60% chance of winning the second match. And success can help you remember facts and concepts.

When male athletes win an event, their testosterone spikes. This gives them a physiological advantage of winning again. Athletes that lose have a very different chemistry in their bodies. So when athletes win, they get an "upward spiral" of testosterone. It should be no surprise if this also happens with cognitive learning.

Success can increase self-efficacy

Self-efficacy is the belief that you or your children have the confidence to successfully learn new and challenging information using the skills they have. You might even call it "level of aspiration"—that is, how they aspire to achieve learning something new. Self-efficacy is an important concept for children to learn new challenges because it gives them the confidence that they will be successful. How do you help your children build self-efficacy? You do this by making their learning successful. In other words, successful past performance is the key. Give them lots of success in a topic.

Use small steps when possible. This book has small steps: for the most part, there are only about three paragraphs under each heading and there are lots of headings and the chapters are short.

Will that help you learn and keep you motivated? Some experts contend that successful small steps have enormous power on the pleasure centers of our brain. Charles Duhigg, in his book *The Power of Habit*, states, "A huge body of research has shown that small wins have enormous power, an influence disproportionate to the accomplishments of the victories themselves." Small wins tend to increase motivation and persistence . . . step by step.

Social consequences

Social consequences can be smiles, praise, and just talking to someone. They are free, they can be delivered easily, and they really light up the pleasure center of your children's brains. Use them every opportunity you have to increase everything from studying, good grades, attention, and persistence.

Review past learning when new facts are learned

There are two major types of factual learning: one is serial learning, like with the alphabet, counting, or learning the names of the presidents in order. The second is stimulus-response learning, where your students match the question (stimulus) with the answer (response). With the alphabet, your children almost always start by saying the letters from the beginning. So they are reviewing and strengthening what they have learned as they add more letters. With stimulus response learning, like when your students learn that the capital city of Tennessee is Nashville, they can be taught the capital city of Oklahoma. When they learn the capital city of Oklahoma, they should be asked the capital of Tennessee again before too much additional stimulus-response learning takes place. And don't forget to take a rest after learning several facts. Also, it's important to review your notes or underline what you have learned when you finish a lesson, and you should review it again before another lesson.

Practice

Review is a form of practice. *Surely, you've heard the saying, "Practice make perfect." That saying has been around longer than*

74

the word "psychology." And it's true. You're making a mistake if you don't make children practice what they have learned, and you do it by having them answer questions within a lesson, and after a lesson . . . and they should do it again with homework. Neurons that fire together wire together and they are stronger and fire longer.

Researchers Larry Coleman and Aige Guo of the University of Toledo in 2014 found that practice played a significant role with children highly passionate to learn. They studied in depth six areas (domains) of passion that these children represented (acting, reading, film making, spelling, math, and preaching). They defined passion as "focused interest which persists over lengthy periods of time and is associated (with a) relative disinterest toward more typical, chronologically aged interests."

Doing intensive interviews, including interviews with parents, they *found that one characteristic of passion that all domains had in common was practice.* For example, the youngster with a passion for mathematics was reading book after book on math and then pouring over the books again and again as if he were over-learning the material. He found this same characteristic to be true for all the selected youngsters. In both of these examples, practice facilitated both the learning of facts and concepts.

Don't Overload Their Brains

Multitasking is what you are doing when you ask your children to learn one thing before it becomes strong enough to be remembered well, and you give them another task to remember. And before the two become strong enough to be remembered, you give them another. You do this enough and you'll cause a complete collapse of what they have learned. That's why you should strengthen the first thing taught before giving the second and strengthen this before the third.

In their book *Algorithms to Live By*, Brian Christian and Tom Griffiths describe a juggler as he hurls only one ball at a time into the air but keeps three aloft by swapping between them quickly enough so that it *appears* to be multitasking. But there is a limit to how much information you can juggle. This is what you do with the telephone number and the program you are watching; it's like the juggler who is juggling three balls. They say, "With one ball in the air, there's enough spare time while the ball is aloft for the juggler to toss some others upward as well. But what if the juggler takes on one more ball than he can handle? He doesn't drop *that* ball: he drops *everything*."

That's exactly the same thing that can happen to your youngsters; give them too much for them to master and they lose it all. That's why they must practice after learning the first fact or concept, practice the first and second after learning the second and this continues on in this fashion as the most remote fact is offered less often. The conclusion is: Don't expect your children to multitask because they can't do it. Give plenty of practice between facts or concepts. Don't overload their brains!

Going Outside your Brain to Remember

No matter how many mnemonics you use or how much you practice, there is a limit as to how much information your brain can hold. Assume you are the ruler of a kingdom of 50,000 people in 30,000 BC. Seven hundred people from a nearby kingdom try to sneak into your kingdom because you have several large bins of grain stored for your people and they were short of food. Can you remember all 50,000 of your people by looking at them and tell those who are not from your kingdom, even if they told you their names? No, your memory has a limit for such things.

According Yuval Noah Harari, author of *Saipan: A Brief History of Humankind, Humans,* humans invented a way to go *outside the brain* to solve problems since the memory could not contain an unlimited amount of information. Between 35,000 BC and 30,000 BC an unknown Sumerian invented a system of recording and storing information outside the brain that could deal with large quantities of information. So this unknown Sumerian invented a way to remember all this information, and today we call it *writing*. This ability to write allowed men and women to coordinate in managing the kingdom and to work together in groups to build roads, bring water to the community, and to determine who and how much property someone owned. Our brains just can't remember all that information without help and writing supplied that help.

You should realize that you cannot remember everything you have read in this book. If you took written notes, made summaries and notations as to the key feature of a concept or chapter, then *you would have gone outside your brain*, just like your ancestors did to help them remember. You have been given a most important gift by the unknown Sumerian. Please use it to help your brain and demonstrate to your children the power of the written word. But you must review the notes in order to remember them.

Reasoning with Facts

Facts are important in reasoning. When children learn to add two column numbers, they must remember to start with the one's column. That's fact! The process of adding is a concept. They are only repeating the rule, It doesn't mean they can actually do the adding. Students can use facts to reason which came first by remembering the dates to the question, "Did Theodore Roosevelt fight as a Rough Rider in the war with Spain over Cuba before or after he was elected president?" Students must recall the dates (facts) and put them in the correct order to answer this question. So reasoning with facts is very important and often used. Encourage your students to use facts to reason through such questions.

Facts are also important in deductive reasoning. For example, if it is a fact the al men are mortal, and if John is a man, therefore he is mortal.

Essence

Be certain to write your summary. Remember, definitions can be facts and knowing them can be helpful in reasoning. Consider using some definitions in your summary.

Reward Yourself

Here's how to note how well you answered the questions according to a standard:

Questions at the beginning of the chapter

5 points for writing the answers to two of the questions given at the beginning of the chapter.

3 points for moving your lips or whispering the answers to two of the questions at the beginning of the chapter.

1 point for thinking of the answers to two of the questions given to you at the beginning of the chapter.

Questions within the chapter

5 points for answering at least three questions within the lesson by writing the answer in your log book.

3 points for answering at least three questions within the lesson by whispering or moving your lips as you said the answers.

1 point for answering at least three questions within the lesson by thinking of the answers.

Essence

Remember the essence is the most important parts of the chapter, not necessarily a summary. By answering the questions given at the first of the chapter, you have probably covered most of the essence and it is not necessary to repeat theses. But add whatever else you considered to be most important.

5 points for writing the essence for the chapter.

3 points for saying out loud or whispering the essence.

1 point for thinking of the answer to yourself.

Compare how you performed as compared to a standard:

Outstanding: 13-15 You certainly deserve being bragged on. Tell yourself you're dedicated to learning to be a super teacher of critical thinking.

Good: 12 This is good work. It's equivalent to a B in some college courses. Tell yourself that you are learning and are going to be able to help children learn critical thinking.

Fair: 9 You're learning and it will show up on the test.

Total your points

You have a possible 75 points. Here's how you did according to the standards of some college professors:
68 or higher, you're in the upper 10 percent.
60-67 you're in the upper 20 percent.
53-59 you're in the upper 30 percent

Bonus!!!!!

If you reviewed your notes even for one or more chapter, you did something very important. So *give yourself 5 extra points* and expect to do well on the test.

Attention for those who did well

For you who scored above 60, you should be very proud of yourself. If anyone makes a perfect score of 75, you are unique and you can mail me at ddickins@utk.edu so I can say something nice about your performance. For those of you who did some of the exercises, you are winners, too, because you will learn more than those readers who are passive, and you will be able to use what you have learned to help your students.

Be a self-managed learner by keeping up your notes and answers in your notebook in the remaining chapters.

Chapter 7
Learning to Think About Thinking

Certainly you want your children to know whether they are thinking logically, reasonably, and that their conclusions make sense. But there some impediments to being logical, reasonable, and sensible with the major one being that their beliefs get in the way. Beliefs are more or less permanent thoughts that are held dearly, strongly, and perpetually. Your students may have them about religion, the value of vaccinations, or even who's the prettiest girl in the classroom. The belief that education and learning are important and are in the best interest of your children will be discussed in this chapter. You will learn how beliefs can be strengthened or changed and this makes a difference in how well your children can think critically.

You would also likely want your youngsters to be enthused about learning instead of having to provide some kind of incentive to entice them to learn. And what about being able to evaluate their school work in an objective way, noting when they need to improve, and taking pride when they have done an effective job? Well, this chapter has some techniques to help you help your children achieve some of these goals, and it is a big step toward critical thinking.

Key Words:
Metacognitive
Beliefs
Rules
Objective
General rule (same as belief)

Q: What direct instruction step could be added that could change your students' beliefs?

Q: How would you insure that your students understand that a reward is the result of doing some specific activities (like using rules to solve problems) and it's something *they did*?

Metacognitive Strategies

Now that you've taught your children how to learn effectively, you can help them to *use the knowledge* they have stored in their heads by employing metacognitive strategies. This term will be used to mean that your students *will take control of their thinking.* They will need to use self-control strategies, monitor how they are doing, correct their reasoning, use the information they have learned to solve problems, and think critically about their thinking with information they are presented. Generally, this is thought to be a "higher-order mental activity" using the prefrontal cortex. (In computer language, they are developing programs to USE their knowledge or data.)

Talking to Ourselves (Thinking)

Since this chapter is about the thinking of children, let's review again the basics about thinking. *Thinking is that verbal dialogue that goes on in your mind all the time.* In other words, it is that talking you do to yourself. We talk to ourselves about all kinds of things all the time, like going to the store, starting a new project, considering what to wear, and thinking about the future and the past. *Some of that thinking propels your children into behaving, and what they say to themselves about their behavior determines whether they repeat it again or not. Their thinking may be a cue to behave, and what they say after the behavior could be a consequence.*

Self-consequence (covert talk)

Self-talk is also a consequence, and it may be a powerful one. We all talk to ourselves and tell ourselves how well we've performed, whether running a race, taking a test, or cleaning the house. *We even talk to ourselves about what we're going to do before we do it,* and this kind of self-talk can make a difference in how your children perform.

Self-talk can occur after a performance and have an effect on the next performance. Self-appraisal should be made to match reality. Youngsters may make high grades on their tests, and you may brag on them for making the high scores. But students may say to themselves, "The teacher made the test easy for me—I'm still a dummy." If that's the self-talk of your students, they have missed the reward of a high score, and that will affect their motivation.

Self-talk can occur before a performance. Some people think about stumbling on a talk to be given at church. They just continue to imagine that they will stumble . . . and that increases the chances that, sure enough, they'll mispronounce the words or forget what they intended to present. Instead, they need to see or rehearse what they are to do as being successful and pleasing to the audience. Even endurance or time to exhaustion can be increased by self-talks. (Yes, you can talk yourself into exercising more!)

Thinking objectively about achievement

If your children are to be effective in adapting to the demands of their environment and think critically about their beliefs, they must first be able to evaluate objectively what they do. Objective means observable and/or measured.

I once took a boy who had years of failure in school on an outing to the mountains. At 8,000 feet, he found some sea shells imbedded in the rocks. When we acted excited and with pleasure about his find, he said to me "You just put it there so I could find it." This youngster had no evidence that I put the shells so he could find it. This was a youngster who had been praised for things he did not accomplish on his own. All children need *objective feedback* on their performance, even high achievers.

Not only do you want your children to realize that they are responsible for their achievement, but the path to responsibility is being able to objectively evaluate their own work. You can do this by having them ask such questions as follows:

- What score did I make last time? Was this better or worse?
- Was my score above or below your average?
- How does that compare with what you wanted?
- Did you make any improvement? How can you tell?

In order to answer these questions, your students must have some data, like grades or test scores. In addition to asking such questions, you can have your children answer the *questions by writing the answers* after inspecting their data.

The importance of data

If your children are to think objectively about how well they are learning, they need some kind of objective data. Data is some kind of *records* like grades, test scores, worksheets, computer records of problems solved, problems missed, or frequency counts that let your students know how they are doing. All the chapters in this section require data. Let your children know the importance of keeping data, how data will help them, and that data can include practice tests so they can make higher grades. Here are some suggestions for collecting data with practice tests:

• Read one or two questions to your children *within a lesson* and have them answer them. Tell students the answers and have them record their accuracy. Do this every day in any subject in which you want improvement. (This can be done with groups.)

• For parents and teachers who have several students, have questions on your homepage that they can answer, grade, and keep a record of their correct and incorrect answers. This can be done within class or after class. If they have laptops, this can be used in class. However, a computer program that rings a bell or gives children a smiley face cannot compete with a parent or teacher who actually looks at what your children have performed.

• Give your children three or four questions to take home to answer before the next class. Give them the answers as soon as they come to class the next day and have them record their accuracy.

• Students can record daily accuracy by computing the percent answered correctly. They can combine days to determine the accuracy during the week.

• Comprehensive tests (for grades or not) can be given once a week and students keep a record of their work.

"You Did It!" How praise should be used
Key Features*:*
• Children need to recognize when *they, themselves,* achieve a goal.

- Children need to be *objective* about what they have done.

Let's assume your students do well on the practice tests. What do you do? Everyone likes a little praise. And *you should be generous with your praise.* Yet, you want your students to furnish their own reinforcement and not be dependent upon praise or other reinforcements from others all the time—you want them to have some intrinsic motivation along with the external rewards. You can get this by *making some of your praise so it impacts on your students' self-talk (or thinking) and is not taken as a reward from you . . . but a reward from themselves.* You can do this when looking at exams, worksheets, answering questions in class, and so on and emphasizing the YOU with such statements as are listed below:

"YOU did it!" Instead of or in addition to "I like that!"
"YOU should be proud of yourself!" Instead of or in addition to "I'm proud of you!"
"That should make YOU feel good!" Instead of or in addition to "That makes *me* happy!"
"YOU should be excited about making a B." Instead of or in addition to "*I'm* happy about that grade!"
"YOU hit the nail on the head with that one!" Instead of or in addition to "That's right!"
"YOU nailed it!" Instead of or in addition to "Nice going!"
"That should make YOU happy!" Instead of or in addition to "That makes *me* happy!"

Note: if you have your students repeat what you have said, like "I did it," after you say, "You did it," it would help to put the thoughts in their heads. Recall that your thoughts can be remembered, so if you can get your students to think, say, or write these words it would be more effective than just telling them that they "did it."

Students Provide their Own Reinforcement

Figure 6   Method for Teaching Students to Use Own Reinforcement

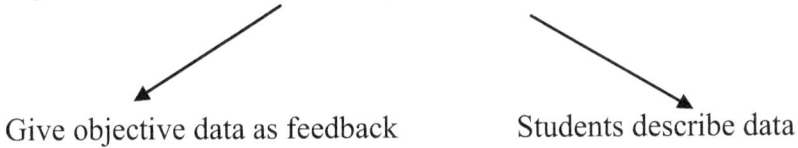

Give objective data as feedback   Students describe data

You want your students to reinforce themselves when they reach a goal instead of depending on you to do the reinforcing by praise or other means. You can change from parent/teacher reinforcement to self-reinforcement by giving objective feedback and having the students describe objectively what they did. You could also add to the teaching of how making an improvement (or reaching a goal) could be beneficial (changing a belief).

Assume that you follow the above steps for getting your students to use the rules recommended in this book. And as a consequence, they do better at learning the material you are teaching. But you want more than this; you want your students to be independent learners. You want your students to transfer the use of these steps when you're not around, like when they are at school, with another tutor, in college, or trying to learn something that reflects their interest.

For all you know, when they follow the rules and you are not around to praise them for their work or give them smiles or chart their progress, they may say to themselves, "What a bunch of crap!" or "I'm tired!" or "It's too much work to use the rules!" or "I'm just plain dumb and without help, I'd never get anything right." If they say these things to themselves, the chance of making a transfer are certainly diminished.

In order to get them to use the rules in other settings, *your students need to learn to find the use of the rules to be reinforcing; that is, the use must stimulate the pleasure centers of their brains in some way.* One way to do this is to teach *them* to *say reinforcing statements to themselves when they reach their goals.*

Using their own words, have your students *describe their work objectively* with statements like:

- That's the third time I have made a B or higher.
- I finally made it! A higher grade!
- An 89! That's improvement!
- I beat my average. Hot dogs!
- Cool, I've made progress by at least 10 percent on every test!

Here's how the parent or teacher does it:

Parent: We've talked about how you could think or say nice things to yourself about your school work; let's start by letting you do these five problems. I'll grade them, and then you tell me how to accurately describe your work.
Parent: (After grading problems.) You got four of the five correct! Now you tell me how you scored?
Student: I got four correct and missed one. That's one better than last time.
Parent: Hey, YOU did improve by one! Give me a high-five and make a smile as big as mine! *(Body language can cause emotions so it's a good idea to make your students act happy when they do something special.)*

What do you do when children *do not make progress*? You have them use the problem-solving coping steps explained in the next two chapters.

Rules and beliefs cause your students to behave

- Key Features: Rules: (sometimes called steps) can be specific to a subject or conduct like rules for doing grammar, mathematics, or table manners.
- Beliefs: are more or less permanent and indisputable ways of thinking like believing immigrants are all harmful to our country.

Rules

Rules can guide your students' conduct and actions. You teach them the rule to add when they see a plus sign and subtract when they see a minus sign. You teach your students all kinds of rules for long-division, algebra, geometry, and even conduct (do not talk without raising your hand). If students say the rules you have taught them to themselves, their covert speech becomes the cue for them to follow the rules—do it enough and it becomes automatic without thinking.

Beliefs

Beliefs are taken as true and undisputable. Beliefs are powerful in controlling your behavior. For many decades, doctors believed that bleeding helped people heal. So when people became ill or the bull kicked them in the head, doctors bled them. If they recovered, the doctors believed the bleeding did it. Of course, some students have rules that don't benefit others. For example, a student may have a belief that is alright to take home anything he finds on the floor (finders' keepers, losers' weepers). Such a belief does not benefit the loser or the keeper in the long run and should be changed.

I once evaluated an elementary-school girl who was having accidents at school. After trying all kinds of things, the teacher referred her to me, thinking there was something mentally wrong since she had already been examined by a physician. When I asked her about the accidents, she told me that she couldn't use the bathroom at school because all public restrooms had germs on the seat. Sooo . . . she tried to hold it the long school day. *You better believe that beliefs are something that one thinks are true.* These beliefs become the cues for behaving and *following them provides satisfaction akin to reinforcement.*

This holds true for the belief in the value of education and those who are responsible for instilling this belief. Some parents believe it is their responsibility to see that their children get the most out of their education—they demonstrate that education is a value to be pursued. They surround them with things that support education, like books and selected videos. They monitor the television viewing in amount and content. And they preach and preach the value of education. They do this early in life so that their children learn these same beliefs. If this happens, the commitment of the children will likely follow because of their beliefs. Beliefs can control a great deal of your children's behavior.

Difference between rules and beliefs

Rules are very specific steps for learning and doing certain tasks while beliefs are more general, undisputable, and may also include rules. Here are some examples:

"Don't touch the figurine" Mother said. "That's the rule."
"Make certain you summarize each paragraph," said the teacher. "That's the rule."
"When subtracting, make certain the upper number is larger than the lower number," said the teacher. "That's the rule." These are all rules (hereafter called reasons) and are very specific.

Beliefs, hereafter called "general reasons" are more general.
"It will benefit us all, if we are honest," said Dad.
"Treat your neighbor as you would treat yourself," said Mom
"Hard work pays dividends," said Grandmother.
"Studying hard, planning, and being persistent are more important than intelligence as measured by an IQ test," said the psychology teacher. (One would *infer that hard work pays dividends*.)

Beliefs are important to critical thinking

You better believe it when you hear that beliefs are important to critical thinking . . . and they are enduring, meaning they are hard to change, especially if you *feel strongly* about them. Whether or not you intend it, you start teaching beliefs before your children open their first schoolhouse door. You teach them about your religion (not all religions), about your political party (not other political parties), whether humans contribute to global warming or not, whether to respect animal life, gun rights, civil rights, fair taxes, compassion, sharing, fairness, and so on. These beliefs become so entrenched that if someone tries to change them, your children will become emotional in defending them. And of course, what they believe causes them to behave in ways that are consistent with their beliefs.

Because beliefs can have strong emotional feelings connected to them, they can interfere with being a critical thinker. As you will see in the chapters that follow, many people tend to distort the facts so they fit their beliefs. That certainly put a damper on thinking critically because you always need evidence if you are going to reach a conclusion about some issues in an *objective manner*. That's why children need to learn early how to *objectively evaluate* the evidence. You'll start with school work (test scores, worksheets, pop quizzes, etc.) in teaching this.

Teaching Thinking of Rules and Beliefs

There's a simple way to modify the thinking of children; you *just teach them to think in a beneficial way.* You want your students to use the rules for reasoning, for self-management, practice, long division, and identifying the critical features of concepts, and you don't want to have to cue them to think about using the rules. You want them to do it automatically, like it is a habit. You've demonstrated how to use the rules, asked them to *verbalize the rules* as they do the problems and then give them feedback—the kind that would increase their use of the rules. *In time you want them to give themselves the type of feedback that would increase or maintain their using the rules. You want them to have the cues in their heads to use the rules and provide their own reinforcement.* You want them to be independent learners.

Writing the reasons for learning and finding help

You already know *learning is enhanced when your students can write* about the lesson more than thinking or talking about it. If you have more than one child to teach at a time, you may need to get your students *to write the rules after making progress on a project or test or after at least maintaining positive standards*. Getting students to write the benefits (general reasons) has also been found to help students. A study published in the *Journal of Science* in 2009 found that when students were asked to *write the usefulness and value of what was being taught* before taking a 10th grade science class, their grades improved over control students who wrote summaries of their studies. In other words, one could infer that writing their values for the course favorably impacted their learning.

Q: What is a general reason? Give an example of a rule and general reason not covered in this chapter.

Teaching rules and general reasons via self-talk

Here's how to commence to teach rules and general reasons (beliefs):

Dad: Listen to me. I'm going to read this page and underline the "who, what, when, where" events, then I'm going make a summary in my own words. I may use mnemonics to help me remember the facts, and I may organize some of the concepts that are different and similar. Then, I'll answer "what if "and factual questions listed in the book. (Dad reads page and does what he says he will do.)

Dad: You know why I followed the rules for studying? (Discussion) Well I did it because I know that following the rules for studying works. I could make higher grades, do my work accurately, and in the long run *I'll benefit from the learning the rest of my life*—and if I were a student that would make my father happy. (General reasons for following rules)

Dad: Now I want you to read this page and pick out the facts that need to be learned . . . use mnemonics if you wish and use the other steps I used. (Son does this.)

Son: Alright, I completed the page and did everything you said. I took the end of chapter test over the concepts on this page and got them all correct.

Dad: Now tell me if you use mnemonics and why?

Son: Yes, I see I could make higher grades if I use the rules of mnemonics.

Dad: Sure! Anything else?

Son: Make you happy.

Dad: Certainly! Now, give me some general reasons that education will benefit you . . .

Son: *It pays to learn.* (General reason)

Remember, a general rule is a belief.

Q: What the difference between a reason and a general reason?

What if the students do not improve or maintain achievement?

If your students do not reach the goals they have set, you will help them to use problem-solving coping. The next two chapters are devoted to this, but here is the essence of what you want your students to do:

• Identify the problem (Not just a low score but exactly what kind of mistakes were made, like multiplication mistakes, using rules incorrectly, not reasoning from a premise, failing to make accurate inferences, and so on. Compare answers to a standard or rules.)

• Develop a strategy to solve the problem and a plan to implement the strategy

Teach reasons for rewards

Social reinforcement has been suggested to be used with teaching, so don't get the idea that such rewards as activities, token reinforcement, or tangibles are always bad! Remember that rewards cause emotional behavior and "emotions stamp the event into memory." Kids get excited about getting rewards, and they pay attention in order to get them. Here's what we know about giving rewards and then removing or reducing the rewards. (Rats will quit responding when you take away the rewards, but sometimes children continue the behavior without the rewards.)

In fact, one study published in *Psychology in the Schools* and later in *Great Experiment in Behavior Modification* found that elementary school children who had token reinforcement, when sent to middle school, gained more on tests of achievement than did the children from three other elementary schools who were sent to the same middle school, and the children from the token reinforcement school had fewer disciplinary problems.

However, most parents and teachers would like to get rid of tangible and activity reinforcement. Most would rather see the children learn because they want to learn. It may take an inch-by-inch approach before this can happen, but it is less likely to happen unless students learn and *believe in the value of learning* and *have enough success to enjoy it.*

Change the mood of your students in just two minutes!

Be aware that you as a parent or teacher play a part in how well your students learn the skills described above. Therefore, you need to use effective instruction as was described and you should be aware that *your mood can affect learning*. And, of course, your students' mood can affect learning.

You will be more effective in teaching the concepts described in this book if your students perceive you as a significant person, someone that they would like to please, and someone whose praise and smiles are reinforcing; if these apply to you, you will have the ability to influence your students' motivation and thinking. Smiling produces endorphins that make the body feel good and smiling releases serotonin (a happy neurotransmitter in the blood stream). By being pleasant and positive you will take a first step in meeting this requirement.

In a study described in David Golman's book, *Emotional Intelligence*, students were brought into a room one at a time where each found another student waiting. The waiting student was an actor unknown to the students. They were both given a checklist on their current mood by an examiner. The examiner left the room for two minutes with the students together facing each other. The actor pretended a good mood for some students and a bad mood for others. Then the two groups of students were given the same questionnaire again after two minutes. *Results were that in just two minutes, the mood of the students could be changed by someone in a bad or good mood* by one's demeanor. Your emotional demeanor can make a difference and set the tone of the classroom or your home. So act happy and be pleasant.

Essence

You have to make a decision here. Are you going to stop answering the questions at this point without the feedback and encouragement or continue by yourself. Are you going to be an independent learner or be dependent on a reward? You won't be sorry if you continue on but you may be sorry if you don't.

Note that combining summering and organizing seems to work better than either one alone. But also notice that it was mentioned above that changing the belief about the value of learning in a science class seems to help children learn more than even summarizing.

Chapter 8
Learning to Problem-Solve

Problem solving is very important to critical thinking . . . but it is not critical thinking. It is a skill your children will need to be effective in critical thinking. When they use critical thinking, they will be using many of the same steps that are used in problem solving, and they will use all the knowledge that they have learned. In fact, when faced with a problem, their brains start searching the areas of their brains that contain similar information to the concepts of the problem.

That's why information is so essential to problem solving . . . but information is not enough to be an effective problem solver; they must be able to use the rules for effective problem solving—like defining the problem, developing strategies, and developing a plan.

It is important to note that all problem-solving strategies use data. It has been found that the use of data is one of the most effective skills that intelligent thinkers can use to make predictions of future events.

Key Words:
Strategies
Structure
Data-based problem solving

Q: What happens to your children's brains when they first start to solve a problem?
Q: Explain why knowledge is important in problem solving?

Learning to Problem Solve

Problem solving is a process to identify, analyze, and solve problems. This process includes discovering and clarifying problems and examining options before taking actions to solve the identified problems. While this chapter will focus on strategies for academic problems for the most part, some examples of social and personal problem solving will also be given. Keep in mind that different kinds of reasoning can be used to solve problems, so some of the strategies listed in this chapter can be used to reason the solution to a problem. Also, keep in mind that *data is an indispensable component of problem solving.*

Figure 7   Using Your Brain to Solve Problems

Steps

1	2	3	4	5
Problem	Seeks Information In schemata	Seeks Additional Information	Rest	Connects with additional schema via synapses

When faced with a problem, your brain looks for information already learned; if the information is not in your head, you must seek additional information, and with the new information, if your brain still cannot solve the problem, have a rest and let the brain reconnect itself.

We know that the first thing children do when faced with a problem is to consult their brains about what they already know about the problem. We know this because brain imagery shows that when children (and all of us) are taught something new, we can see where the new information is filed in their brains (because that area of the brain being used lights up in imaging software). Then if given a problem to solve that they have never faced before, their brain scans show that the children immediately go to the relevant material that was just learned. That's evidence they are using their brains!

When being *creative and inventing* new scientific information, Louis Pasteur once said that "...chance favors the prepared mind." That means you're more likely to be an effective problem solver, be creative, or be a discoverer if you have relevant information already stored in your mind . . . you're prepared. (Creativity is having a fluency of ideas, for without ideas you could never solve a problem.) And don't think that the Wright brothers just came to an idea out of the blue to build a contraption that would fly and carry a man. No, they wrote a letter to the Smithsonian asking for all the books and papers in their possession on the possibility of flying. When they received them they read them. Then they watched birds. Really, they became bird watchers and learned how birds maintained stability when flying. The Wrights copied in their flying machines what the birds did. They prepared their minds for the discovery of the first aircraft.

Examples of using knowledge

Having access to all the information in a schema filed neatly away in your brain would certainly aid in problem solving. You may have filed several examples of problems you have solved in your brain, although they may not be exactly alike. When faced with solving the problem of predicting how global warming will impact butterflies in Korea by June 2025, you will need to pull out of your brain not only examples of how to solve problems, but also information about the climate in Korea, what kinds of butterflies are there, habitat for butterflies found in Korea, information about butterflies in general, and something about global warming. So you need to have learned the information, and you need to be able to retrieve it so you can use it. *If you haven't already learned the information, you must access it someplace else, like in a book or a video. Once it is recorded in your gray matter, you can use it.*

In 2011 Feng Zang had a problem: he was trying to "edit cells from mammals." He had been working at the Massachusetts Institute of Technology and at Harvard University's Board Institute to develop a way to cut and paste DNA. He had a great deal of information in his head about genomes and editing cells, but he still could not solve the problem. He just happened to attend a lecture on how bacteria can clip out sections of DNA. He added that information to his existing knowledge to solve the problem of editing cells from mammals. Other scientists could not have discovered how to use bacteria to clip sections of DNA because they had different sets of knowledge. They did not have "prepared minds." Having just the right knowledge is essential for problem solving.

Problem-Solving Strategies

Key Features:

- A *strategy* is a method for achieving some objective--use your hands to milk the cow (Strategy 1) or use an electric milking machine (Strategy 2).
- A *plan* is the steps on how to get where you want to go. (A plan to milk the cow is the steps of the strategy (feed the cow, get a pail and stool, put the bucket under the cow etc.) These concepts are often used interchangeably and some strategies need no plan.

A problem-solving strategy is a method for achieving some objective. A problem-solving strategy occurs with *a plan* once the problem has been defined (like you did with critical features of concepts). This should already be in your brain from reading the chapters on concepts. There are all kinds of problem-solving strategies.There are too many problem-solving strategies to mention them all but listed below are some popular problem-solving strategies for academics.

Learning from errors

Certainly, you would like your students to learn without errors. It's not going to happen. Woody Allen was once asked if he had gotten wiser as he had gotten older. He replied something like, "Heck no! I keep making the same dumb mistakes as I made when I was young!" You would think that we would benefit from knowing our errors of youth and not repeat them. We should, but it depends on how we handle the errors whether we benefit from them. There are several strategies to help your children learn from errors.

Here's a strategy for solving a problem using the technique of *systematically recording errors.* Assume you lose something in your home. You generally use a systematic search, like going to the most likely place or last place you remember having the object (strategy) and search that room. Then you go to another room, then another, one by one before repeating going to the most likely place again. Surely you have done this if you've lost your glasses. You remember where you've already looked (errors) and try not to repeat them before completing a systematic search.

With school subjects the same would be true. *Keeping track of errors and comparing these errors with problems in which no errors were made is a basic step to benefiting from errors. Even comparing one's work with illustrations or definitions can be beneficial when errors are made.* These are problem-solving strategies. With a record of errors, students are learning how to store information of their errors just like Thomas Edison did when trying to find how to develop a more effective incandescent electric light. He was once asked why he didn't give up after a thousand failures. He replied that he didn't have a thousand failures; he had just learned a thousand ways it would not work.

Looking for structure (form of inductive reasoning)

When you use critical thinking, you are trying to make sense out of your world. Information that does not fit, like the absence of the critical features of a concept, will cause you to reject your conclusion. Looking for structure is an essential part of critical thinking and problem solving.

Keep in mind that *the goal of science is to understand, predict, and control.* If we understand the phenomena, we may then predict what will happen in the future, and then we may be able to control events. By finding structure, it helps your students to learn and predict.

Most of us believe *there is a pattern or structure to our world.* Scientists are always looking for this structure. If your students are working by themselves, learning is enhanced if they can detect that what they are learning has a pattern—even a mathematical pattern. Starting with preschool, youngsters are given items and asked to determine which are alike and which are different. That's an example of finding structure. Look at the example below. This describes a lesson in grammar. If you can teach your students to look for this structure (or rule) and teach them to test out their beliefs about the structure when they make errors, you will be teaching them a strategy for problem solving.

The girl *lives* in a red house.
The girls *live* in a red house.
The boy *lives* in a white house.
The boys *live* in a white house.

There have been several research projects that have found that teaching students to look for structure, patterns, and sequencing leads to higher achievement in school subjects. In a study that used the examples of grammar given above, elementary students were taught to find the structure of their lessons. The lessons consisted of several presentations of numbers that were to be added or multiplied, as well as language exercises. Students were taught to find the patterns to their assignments.

At the end of the school year, it was found that the group with the instruction on finding structure to their lessons had increased scores on tests of creativity over a control group. They had learned a problem-solving approach (a fluency of ideas). Some psychologists consider this to be a lesson on *discovery learning*.

With math, your students can find a great deal of structure. One of the most apparent examples is with the multiplication of numbers differing by five:

1x5=05
2x5=10
3x5=15
4x5=20

Knowing this structure, a student can predict what 5x5 would be. Note that the last digit *of the product alternates between 0 and 5 and the first number is repeated twice and of course the* product increases by 5—even more structure. Math has all kinds of structure. When the pattern is discovered, one would then reason what the next number would be. *That's inductive reasoning*, and you might conclude that the next number is *likely* 25. (With inductive reasoning, you never conclude that the conclusion is absolute.)

When your children take their toys apart or when you take your watch apart, you are both looking to see how it works . . . that is the same as looking for structure. Biologists who are studying the impact of environmental warming on plant life are looking for the structure (relationship) between plant growth and temperature. Psychologists who are studying the impact of learning to read at an early age are looking for the structure so they can understand, predict and make interventions to help children.

Q: What is meant by "looking for structure?"

Working backward (backward reasoning)

There are many times that problems can be solved by reducing them into parts. Working backward is a technique that starts with the end and works in steps to the beginning. Here's an example:

Marianna drove from Nashville to Murfreesboro in 2 hours and 50 minutes. Then it took her 50 minutes to drive from Murfreesboro to Smyrna. She arrives in Smyrna at 3:00 PM. What time did she leave?

Problem: What time did Marianna leave Nashville?

Problem-solving strategy: working backward

Plan: Start by determining how long it took her to get to Smyrna from Murfreesboro (50 minutes) and then subtract the time it took her to go from Murfreesboro (2 hours and 50 minutes) to Nashville. This should give the time she arrived (3:00 P.M).

Subtract 50 minutes from 3:00 = 2:10

Subtract 2 hrs. and 30 minutes from 2:10 = 11:40 P.M.

Check:

Started at 11: 40

11:40+ 50 minutes = 12:30 +2 hrs. and 30 minutes= 3:00 PM

Data-based problem solving (Make a table or chart)

Data describing precisely what students do is more valuable in helping to solve problems than obtaining the labels, group names (Blue Birds), or a diagnosis of children (mentally challenged). It's more useful to say that a youngster does not know his "9 times" than to say he is learning disabled. Data can also be valuable in solving problems. Data can be presented in charts, figures, tables, or records

100

of other kinds. Figures have been used in most chapters to allow you to get visual mental pictures of the contents. Notice that the table below can be used to denote what the next data point would be.

Question: You save $6 on Monday. Each day after that you save twice as much as you saved the day before. If this pattern continues, how much would you save on Friday?	$6
Monday	
Tuesday	$12
Wednesday	$24
Thursday	$48
Friday	$96

You saved $96 by Friday.

Solving prediction problems with the average rule

Predictions can be a challenging problem. You don't know the future, and it's often difficult to predict. Over the years people have made some useful observations as to how to make predictions, like "the best predictor of future behavior is past behavior" and "how you spend today is likely how you will spend the rest of your life."

Mathematics can be very useful in making predictions. Here's an example from Christian, B. & Griffiths, T. in their book *Algorithms to Live By*. Using the average rule is a very common strategy for making predictions. Assume you are someone from Mars and you know nothing about people on earth. The first person you meet is a man dressed in clothes. He wears a hat and shoes. He looks strange to you with his body covered. You asked him how old he is and he says 90. So you figure out quickly by doubling the number that he would live to be 180. But another person on earth comes along and tells you that's impossible because he has more information. This person knows that longevity has a *normal distribution* and if plotted, a large number of people would be in the middle of the distribution and there would be fewer and fewer as the distribution trails off above and below the center or average. You can use this distribution to find out how long the 90-year-old man is expected to live by simply looking at the distribution of longevity for 90-year olds and determining the average. That average of 4 years would be your best estimate because half of the 90-year-olds are already dead and half still remain alive in 4 years.

Sleepy-time solutions

Sleep and relaxation can help with problem solving. What about those crazy dreams? You find yourself wandering in a town you don't recognize, but people you know are there, and all of a sudden, they're gone. You start running and you run so fast that you start to fly. Or you might dream you're going to take a test and you haven't read a chapter for the text and haven't even been to class the entire semester. Would you believe those dreams are really good for you? Yes, dreaming is good for you. You're relaxed and so is your brain, but it continues to operate. Because the dendrites and other supporting fiber help make the connections to other neurons so you can connect to other schema recorded in your head, when you relax, these connections among schema just jiggle all over your brain, and that's why you have such crazy mixed-up dreams.

But there's more! When you relax and sleep, your brain solidifies what you have learned and makes it stronger. Generally, you will be able to recall more the next morning. Sleep and relaxation even help you with problem solving. A Harvard University psychologist, Deirdre Barrett, found that when students were given a problem to dream about, nearly half of the students did dream about the problem . . . and a quarter of them found the answer in their dreams.

Not only do dream states help you solve problems, but also just relaxing your brain by walking or engaging in some enjoyable activity help. Sleep can also have an impact on students' grades. Kids getting 15 minutes more of sleep get higher grades than those making B's. Kids making B's get 15 minutes or more of sleep than those making C's.

Rules for Problem Solving

Key Features:
- Clearly identify the problem you want to solve using data.
- Develop one or more strategies with a plan (steps for the strategy).
- Collect information (data) on the problem.
- Use what information you already know and collect more if needed.
- Implement your strategy plan.
- Evaluate. (Check to see your progress in solving the problem.)

Listed below are the components of problem solving. You need to first show and tell your students how to follow the six steps.

Rule 1 Identify the problem so it can be measured.

Identify the problem so it can be seen/heard and measured. It is important to fully *define the parameters of the problem* or goal in such a way that it can be solved and you can evaluate success. That generally requires *having some kind of data* or record to see how you're progressing or determining if the problem is solved.

If you get a note from your child's teacher saying she needs to increase her grades from an average of C to an average of B, you'll be better off to use test scores (like the percentage of errors) to clarify what is a C or B grade using quantifying data, like the actual scores or percentage of correct answers. Grades can be useful, too, but having more precise measurements would be more helpful. You can also define the problem as a goal, like "Mary will increase her grades from a 75 to 85 average by the end of four months."

When a problem has been identified, have your students verbalize the problem to make certain they fully understand it. If your students have difficulty doing this, have them make a diagram or a figure of the problem. Some math problems may require this in order to obtain a complete definition of the problem.

Rule 2 Develop one or more strategies.

When you identify a problem or a goal, you can think of ways to solve the problem. (You might consider a couple of strategies to reach the goal.) A strategy is what you think will solve the problem; like when one of your children is making low grades, you might have a strategy to increase the youngster's *study time* (Strategy 1) or to require your youngster *to use effective study skills* (Strategy 2) like the comprehension skills listed in previous chapters. Then you must decide which strategy is most likely to work and start with that after developing a plan.

Develop a plan to use the strategy

Strategies must have plans for effective implementation. The *plans should have steps* to get your students from where they are to where they want to go. If you select the strategy for using direct instruction to teach your youngsters the times tables, the first step of a plan might be to find out what times tables your children know and do not know. Your steps could also include the reviewing of what has already been learned before you introduce new times tables, as was described in the teaching of facts.

Rule 3 Collect information on the strategies

Key Features: You collect information by:
- Use *information in your head.*
- Collect *new information* (and put it in your head).
- *Determine (monitor) how you are performing* by getting a baseline (for some problems).

Baseline

For students who do not complete their homework, a baseline of their work would also be helpful. *A baseline is a measure taken before they start their problem-solving program.* It can also give you some idea of what the problem is as well as what the solution might be. For the problem of low grades, you would need to collect current test scores and continue to collect them during the intervention. Let's assume you receive a phone call from Mr. Singer saying your daughter is not doing her homework. Here's how the dialogue could go:

Dad: Thanks for letting me know, Mr. Singer. Could you tell me a little more about Janice's homework? How often does she not turn it in?

Mr. Singer: Well she turns it in almost every day. I give homework three times a week. The problem is she doesn't complete it. I give her a social studies assignment to read and answer questions in response to the reading.

Dad: So the problem is that she's not completing the questions. Does she attempt to answer any of the questions?

Mr. Singer: Yes, she answers some.

Dad: Are they correct?

Mr. Singer: Yes, for the most part. She may answer the first three or four and not try to answer the others.

Dad: Do you have her scores on the questions?

Mr. Singer: Yes, she's averaging about 50% for the three last weeks and only 30% for the week before.

Dad: So it appears that I need to help her to finish her homework assignments; is that correct?

In this scenario the problem has been clearly defined, a baseline is already available, and a clear way to measure it has been found.

Use what is in your head

Before you collect a great deal of information on how to solve the problem, use the information you already have in your brain to test out a solution. In this step you can rattle around in your brain to see what's in there that may help you. For the Korean butterfly problem, you need information to solve a problem, and the first place to start is with what you already know. The same thing might be true for increasing your youngster's homework scores by increasing the amount of time she spends doing her homework, since you've already read about the relationship of study time and grades. Your youngster's teacher may have already told you that your daughter turns in less than half of her homework, and that's recorded in your head.

Collect more information

If you do not have the information, you need to seek it from books or other sources and put it in your head in a meaningful way just like the example with the butterflies in Korea. For the homework problem, you could refer to books on motivating children or you might conclude that you need to teach your daughter self-management strategies or you could ask her teacher to give less homework, but you reject this as a bad strategy as you know the reputation of Mr. Singer (using information to reject or reason about a strategy).

Use your head to test the strategies (reasoning)

As you build a strategy, you can sometimes test it in your head without ever doing an actual test. This is the step that makes us different from other species. We can set up an experiment *in our minds and test it out without actually doing it.* We *test it out by reasoning*, based on the information we have, like saying to ourselves, "If I mix salt in water, it will dissolve? I don't want that to happen, so I'll try something else." If your strategy is to increase your daughter's study time, use what you already know about getting your daughter to do things that seem to work, like using a contingency.

Rule 4 Develop a plan and implement the most promising strategy.

After collecting some information on each of the strategies, you should select one that is considered to be most likely to work. Now you are ready to try your problem-solving strategy and plan. Assume you decide to *use a strategy of seeing if your daughter starts her homework earlier enough to complete it.* As your plan you could:

- Have her bring her work to you when she is finished or at bedtime.
- If it is not finished at bedtime, you have her start her

homework 15 minutes earlier the next day.
- If this works, get feedback from the teacher to make certain the answers are to the teacher's standard. If correct, you have solved the problem.

Rule 5 Evaluate the results.

Effective problem solvers tend to monitor their progress as they work toward solutions. If your students are not making acceptable progress toward reaching their goals, they should reevaluate their approaches or look for new strategies.

Does it make sense?

When your students reach solutions, they should examine the solutions to make certain they make sense. They can ask themselves the question, "Is the problem really solved, and did the monitoring do the trick?"

When finished teaching the rules to your students, have them state the most important steps for problem solving (define the problem, develop a strategy and plan, collect more information if necessary, and implement and evaluate the plan). Then have them state the general rule like, "Using the steps to problem solving will help me solve all kinds of problems."

Reasoning

There's a great deal of reasoning going on in problem solving. Problem solving covers cause-and-effect (scientific), reasoning by inferences, by connecting the dots (finding structure,) and backward reasoning.

Essence

Keep finding the essence for your notes if you want to increase your learning. Most often you can do this by answering the first two questions at the beginning of the chapter. This is a prompt and prompts work. Let's see if it works with you.

Chapter 9
Learning to Cope

Everyone gets frustrated sometimes, so how you cope makes a big difference in whether or not you solve a problem. Many children use emotional coping when faced with stress, like blaming others or becoming angry. What you should want your children to do is to recognize that they can solve problems more effectively by using problem-solving coping. This even works for situations that have no solution. Sound impossible? It's not.

Sometimes your children can learn to use both emotional and problem-solving coping at the same time, like learning to laugh at their mistakes (to make them feel better) and at the same time trying to solve the problem (finding out why they made mistakes). Your children can become problem-solving coppers by learning effective methods for coping.

Key Words*:*
Problem-solving coping
Maladaptive coping
Emotional coping

Q: Why is problem-solving coping more valuable than emotional coping?
Q: What are the steps for problem-solving coping?

Two Types of Coping

Key Features:
* Problem-solving coping (Using the steps of problem-solving along with coping to solve problems.)
* Emotional coping (Using emotional techniques to make children feel better or to cope with a problem that they cannot solve or think they cannot solve.)

First, let's start with a definition of coping and some examples of problem-solving coping and emotional coping . . . or a combination of the two. *Coping is a method of responding to frustration or a blocked goal.* You've probably seen many youngsters who are frustrated because they do not get what they want. They will pitch temper tantrums by falling to the floor, crying, and sometimes vomiting. These kids are frustrated and trying to cope with a blocked goal—and that's called emotional coping.

On the other hand, you've seen children who, whenever they encounter a blocked goal—like trying to understand the instructions for doing a history lesson—follow problem-solving coping. They first must admit that they have the problem of understanding the instructions. Then they develop strategies to help them understand the instructions. One strategy might be telling themselves to reread the instructions and to note whether there are different parts or steps to the instructions. If they still don't understand, they might seek help from teachers or parents. Problem-solving coping certainly beats having tantrums or blaming teachers.

Now that you have an idea of problem-solving coping and emotional coping, let's define the two and give you the steps or examples of each. *Problem-solving coping is following the steps of problem solving, as mentioned in the last chapter.* You define the problem, have ideas (strategies) on how to solve the problem, and try them out to see how your ideas work by collecting data. Emotional coping is trying to reduce the stress, like anger or frustration. It makes you feel better, but it does not solve the problem.

Sometimes you may use a combination of the two. Emotional coping like taking deep breaths, counting to 100, or thinking about something else, may calm you down and help you get your wits back so you can use problem-solving coping. Emotional coping, in some instances, may continue for a long time unless the problem is solved. Here's an example of using the two together over a period of time:

Using emotional and problem-solving coping together

In 2014 the *New York Times* published a story about a youngster who was autistic. He was teased, called retarded and other hurtful names, and was the butt of jokes. He solved the problem, not by becoming angry, but by joining in on the jokes to soften the

110

teasing and to make friends. He struggled to become a more effective learner (problem-solving approach) while laughing at himself. As a grown man he has now written several books and has written of his experiences. His articles were published by the *New York Times*. While also doing his residency as a medical doctor—he lived through the unsolvable by managing his autism.

Many people have learned to use emotional coping and problem-solving coping together. You may have made mistakes before when giving a cashier the correct change. But instead of blaming the cashier, you smile or laugh and say to yourself such things as "I'll be a little more careful this time" or "Let me see what the correct cost is and how best to make change." You do such things all the time. You use both emotional and problem-solving coping.

Q: Why is problem-solving coping superior to emotional coping?

Making emotional coping into problem-solving coping

When there is no possibility of using problem-solving coping to solve a problem, like when you are going blind and there is no cure, you could use emotional coping by blaming the doctors or your parents or spouse for not finding the eye problem earlier. You could tell yourself that it won't be so bad to be blind, you could sue the hospital, or you could spend your time sending hostile messages on the web about your situation. Or you could simply change your thinking.

Your change of thinking might be to approach this situation using the problem-solving model to find the most effective way to make an adjustment to being blind, like learning Braille, working with a sightseeing dog, or learning how to use voice recognition software on your computer to print. In other words, you could teach your children to make the unsolvable problem into a problem-solving method to help make the best adjustment possible. Parents and teachers, you do this by modeling your thinking . . . out loud.

Academic and Social Coping

There are all kinds of stressors in your world, and they require different way of adjusting to them; however, this chapter deals with only academic and social stressors that are likely to happen at school.

According to Dr. Jann Cupp, coauthor of the *Academic and Social Coping Inventory* (ASCI,) students who do well coping with academic stress also do well with social coping. He developed a scale to determine whether students used problem-solving coping (similar to those used in problem-solving) or emotional coping (like withdrawing, becoming aggressive, blaming others, making light of the incident, and so on) when faced with stress at school. His scale used student behaviors that teachers had nominated. Here are some questions from the ASCI that *measure academic coping* on a five-point scale using teacher ratings:

When/if the student makes a low score, he/she does such things as:
1 _____ Withdraws, has nothing to do with others.
2 _____ Pouts, cries, throws a temper tantrum or refuses to do work.
3 _____ Works on another task completely unrelated to the problem, like drawing instead of   working math problems.
4 _____ Blames others for his/her low score.
5 _____ Asks a teacher/peer to help him/her improve performance or seeks support.
6 _____ Asks what he/she did wrong.
7_____ Develops such strategies as re-reading, being prepared, or using reference material and/or tries different ways to solve problem.
8_____ Follows a plan he/she has developed to solve the problem and improve.

You can see that the first question evaluates whether withdrawal is used, the second measures aggression or emotional outburst, and the fourth evaluates projection (blaming others). The next four questions measure problem-solving coping. These are: asking for help, determining the cause of errors, determining how to solve the problem, and following a problem-solving plan. Asking for help should be done last except when asking for clarification of the problem. There are many examples of emotional coping, like making fun or joking about the problem, thought switching (thinking about something else), and so on. Of course you would want your students to use the problem-solving strategies.

There were also questions on the ASCI about how children adjust in social situations like "When/if the student fails to get his/her own way when sharing or playing, he/she does such things as: . . .."

We like to blame others

In an unpublished study by Michelle Dawson, Lorie Beller, Lynn Churchman, and Karen Loy, researchers using the ASCI found that the most frequent emotional coping used by students was to blame others (projection). You might reflect for a moment to think how often you use this method. I am reminded of using it when some of my books are misplaced; I immediately ask my wife if she moved my books. Almost always she says no, and later I find I had moved them. Also, children with emotional problems seem to have the most problems using problem-solving coping, even more than children with a learning disability.

Blaming others is not an effective way to cope. After committing a crime, the method of coping has been found to be a predictor of whether the person will likely commit a crime after being released. *That is, those who blame others are more likely to get in trouble again.* That's a shame because projection is so often used. When children use projection, try to get them to use reasoning to think through the sequence of how they believe others contributed to their mistakes. Then have them determine *their* parts in making the mistakes. See an example of using data and "You did it" in the rules below.

They must believe

Your students should believe that they can solve or improve their problem solving and coping *before they will likely use the rules for problem-solving coping.* How do you make them believe that they can solve problems? You give them enough success to develop

113

some confidence that they can succeed. This comes about because you taught them to be *objective about evaluating their work* and to *use verbal statements* that fit the objectivity of their performances, to learn the *rules* for learning whether it is mathematic fractions or the organization of a term paper. Having your children think, talk, or write to themselves can help them use self-control, manage emotions, and deal with stress. This is sometimes referred to as self-regulation.

Teaching Academic and Social Coping

In this section, you will read about ways to teach your children to cope with failure, anxiety, and stress in academic and school-social situations. The very first step in teaching coping is to provide the rationale for learning to cope.

Rationale

Let your children know how their brains work. Let them know that stress and frustration are natural when they face blocked goals or disappointments. Show them how the brain detects what might be threats by signaling their bodies to be prepared for fight or flight. Explain how the brain sounds an alarm that sends adrenaline through the body, sending blood to muscles and increasing heart rate. Of course, to problem solve, one must calm down in order to use the prefrontal cortex—the part of the brain used for reasoning. Students may do this by take deep breaths, relaxing, and telling themselves to calm down before attempting to define the problem.

Provide your children with slides, pictures, and diagrams that better explain this process so they will see that it is natural to get emotional and that emotional reactions can be controlled with practice. You can use the *Brain Works Project*, California Department of Education for more information, including pictures on how the brain functions while coping with stress. See it at: https://www.youtube.com/watch?v=3bKuoH8CkFc

Also, review the difference between problem-solving coping and emotional coping. For high school students, you could have them read the description from this book. For younger children you

114

could give *examples* from this book. Make certain all your children understand and can repeat the basic steps for problem-solving coping:

- Define the problem.
- Develop one or more strategies for solving the problem.
- Evaluate the effectiveness of the strategy.
- Ask for help.

Modeling

One of the most effective methods for teaching most anything is to demonstrate the concept by showing and telling. Parents and teachers have a wonderful opportunity to model how to cope by using *self-talk*. For example, if you misplace your glasses or purse, you should tell your children, "Now I've got a problem here. My problem is that I'm in a hurry and I can't find my glasses. I have an appointment in just a few minutes, and I just can't be late. I need to take a deep breath and calm down just a few seconds so I can think. My strategy to find my glasses would be to look where I last remember using them . . . and that was in the bedroom while reading the newspaper. Let's see if that works."

You should also demonstrate how to cope with errors (or unknown information) while you are teaching. You do this by pausing to think before coming to a conclusion, evaluate what you are saying, and using the problem identification, intervention strategy, and an evaluation method of problem solving. Now you may not think that teaching is stressful, but just consider that you are teaching a class of 30 students and they think you know everything and you are perfect, and you make a mistake; you may not recognize it, but your brain knows it and is likely to send a threat message to your body. Here are a couple of short examples of demonstrating problem-solving coping.

Focus on the problem definition. (Err . . . I think "social" means being around people . . . wait, that's a little narrow because people can talk to others and even see them on Skype . . . so I'd better use the dictionary to define this.)

Make correction and practice. (Err . . . so the dictionary says "social" means relating to an organization or community . . . it could also mean gregarious or interactive . . . well, I'd better check the context to see what the meaning is.)

When you use problem-solving coping, you are actually demonstrating how to make mistakes and correct them.

Scenarios

Another way to teach coping is to use scenarios and have your students answer questions about the scenarios. Teach them to pause and relax a minute before trying to define the problem, develop a strategy, and evaluate how they are working. Here's an example of a problem that will show you how to develop other strategies that are age appropriate:

Sheri's mother gets a note from Sheri's teacher showing her test scores in science as 58, 75, 44, and 60. Sheri's mother shows the scores to Sheri and asks: "What's going on?"
Sheri is embarrassed, so what should she do first?
What is the problem?
What strategy could Sheri use to cope with the problem?
How could Sheri tell whether her strategy worked or not?

Problem-Solving and Coping Self-Talk with Blocked Goals

When students are blocked from achieving their goals, here are some self-statements that they could use to help them cope with their school work:

Questions students should ask themselves:

- What did I do wrong? (problem-solving coping)
- Let me go back to the directions to see if I understood.
- Let me compare what I did with the definition or with the steps.

- I could check with my book or a reference book or ask someone for help.
- I can see there's no way to solve this problem so I must figure out the best way to live with it (emotional coping morphs into problem-solving). Since I can't solve this problem, let me think of a plan to live with it (make the best of it).
- I'll think of something positive (thought switching).

Have your students summarize with general-reason statements. (Problem-solving is the most effective way to face problems.)

How to Use Problem-Solving Coping

When teaching problem-solving coping by demonstrating in the classroom or home, you should let your students hear your thinking as you obtain an answer to a question. Instead of just showing and telling how to determine the answer, as was recommended in the chapter on learning concepts, you demonstrate how to work through problem solving as if you were figuring out the answer. Assume you are teaching the concept of "justice," which is an abstract concept. Here's how the dialogue might go.

"Alright everyone, today we're going to study what is meant by 'justice' and what are the differences between justice and similar concepts like fairness. Let me . . . Okay! We have a problem here . . . seems like there are several definitions . . . depending on what kind of justice were talking about. What am I going to do? Just quit? Give up and go on to something else? No, I'll try to use a problem-solving approach.

"I know what my problem is now. I need an accurate definition of justice. Since I don't have the information in my head, I must find information someplace else. Let me look in the dictionary. It says that the word could be *justice under the law*? Or it says the term could mean an agreement *that's fair for all people*. Hmm . . . we need to pick one . . . let's go with the definition *under the law*. It reads 'The process or result of using laws to fairly judge and punish crimes and criminals.'" (The lesson continues.)

117

Example of problem-solving coping with math

In order to teach your students to become effective problem solvers, you must first demonstrate how to be an effective problem solver . . . and you must do it time and time again. You can do it with the teaching of concepts, you can do it when thinking about planning a lesson, you can do it when one of your students loses her book, you can do it with any problem that you are faced with when tutoring your students. Show and tell the children how to use the steps of problem-solving coping when reading, doing math, and even when teaching them how to find the critical feature of concepts.

The following is an example of a parent using a problem-solving and coping model for doing long division with a middle-school girl. The steps modeled were problem identification, developing a plan to utilize the rules for solving the problem, and evaluation. The parent models coping by making mistakes when estimating how many times 9 goes into the dividend and then correcting the mistakes.

Parent: Let's see what you're supposed to do? This is your homework. Page 109, I can see that these are long division. I need to think about it just a minute (*problem identification*). We're going to use some rules to solve these problems . . .it seems like . . . the first rule would be to check to see if the divisor is equal to or smaller than the first number (*plan*). I'm going to divide 9 into 36 . . . I see if my divider is larger . . . I can't divide 9 into 3 . . . so I divide 9 into 36. How many times will 9 go into 36 or what number times 9 will equal 36? I'm going to try 5. Nine times 5 equals 45. I need a smaller number. I'll try a smaller number (*coping*), again, I'll try 4 . . . 4 times 9 equals 36. Is that right? Yes. (*Evaluation*) This time it's 9 into 81. . . 9 will not go into 8 . . . so, I take 9 into 81. I'll try 10 . . . 10 times 9 equals 90. That doesn't work. I'll try 9 times 7 . . . it goes. Nine times 9 equals 81 (*coping*) . . . let me check that, 9 times 9 equal 81 with no remainder. So I must be doing it right (*evaluation*).

Example of coping while teaching to look for structure

When you demonstrate how to problem solve as described in the last chapter, you need to show how to use a strategy. Assume you are a parent of a preschool child or early first or second-grade youngster; here's how you would demonstrate using the strategy of structure and problem-solving coping together:

Parent: Alright Alexi, look at these words. I'm going to show you how to look for the structure (similarity or likeness) with the words below. I'll ask myself how they are alike. If I can find out how they are alike, I may be able to make a new word that sounds like the first three. Bat, hat, mat, at. Well let me see. They are all three-letter words, so I'm going to see if they have any of the same letters. Let me see . . . maybe they *start* with the same letter . . . no they don't. They start with b, h, and m. So I should look at the *last* letter. Yes, they all end in *"t."* They all end in "at" and the endings sound alike. So I could use other letters like "a," no . . . won't work, "b", no won't work, . . . I know one . . .cat . . . does "cat" make the same "at" sound like the others? Yes, yes.

After teaching your children how to cope when they make mistakes or solve a problem, have your students state a general rule like, "I need to use problem-solving coping again to try to correct my mistakes or try to find the most useful way to adjust to something I can't change."

Problem-Solving Coping Rules

The problem-solving coping rules borrow some of the rules that were used for problem solving as well as some of the rules for other skills. Obviously, your students will need to start with recognizing that they are faced with problems.

Rule 1 Recognize a problem

Your children must recognize when *they* have problems. They must accept them as *their problems* and not blame their teachers or parents. The most effective way to demonstrate when they have problems is to use data. Get your youngsters to review their test scores (objective data) first. If they can identify problems it is more likely they will take ownership of the problems. Do this by reviewing the data and using reasoning. If that doesn't work, you could say something like this, "Rendell, let's examine how you are doing on our weekly tests. Notice that four weeks ago when we started looking at the causes of World War II, your had scores of 55, 70, 60, 44, and 72. What does that mean?" Whatever approach you use, try to get your children to recognize that they have problems and use the data to clearly define them.

For the most part, examples have been given of continuous data, like a series of test scores; but there are other types of data that would help with problem solving and coping, like historical events.

Rule 2 Develop and implement strategies

You should try to get your students to use their knowledge in selecting one or more strategies for solving their problems. They should already know the rules for comprehension, learning facts, telling one concept from the other, how to practice, and so on. They should be encouraged to use such knowledge to solve problems. For example, the student with low scores in geography may say, "I'll try to use the rules for comprehension more effectively by making a summary after each topic heading. That will be my strategy." *Then a plan should be developed* and followed as the student implements the strategy.

Rule 3 Evaluate

Data certainly helps if you are evaluating your progress, especially data that is continuous. That is, if you have baseline data and intervention data for several days, that would be most helpful. With this kind of data, you can compare how students score before the intervention and after the intervention. But some problems do not call for continuous data, like trying to find your glasses. In such cases you rely on historical data. For example, you may have lost your glasses before and have used the searching techniques of asking yourself where you last used them. You would use that historical information to reason how to find your glasses.

Rule 4 Seek help
It is getting easier and easier for you and your children to get help. You cope with a problem not by giving up, but as a last resort, seeking help. That help can come from parents, teachers, or peers. It can come from books, magazines, or the internet. There's even help from your phone and even such electronic devices as Google Home.

Reasoning:

Since children should use a problem-solving method of coping instead of an emotional method, they would be using many of the same reasoning methods as with problem solving. For example, when they see they are not achieving their goals, they would reason by comparing what they did with their plans to see what aspects they did not follow (criteria reasoning). If they find nothing wrong, they could reason about their plans being inaccurate (conditional reasoning—if . . . then …). Also, looking for structure is a type of analytical reasoning, as in trying to find a pattern so one can predict.

Essence
If you are going to teach your children the steps for problem-solving coping, how can you do it without knowing the steps for coping? Everyone of them!

Chapter 10
Learning Self Management

You teach your children how to organize information so it fits the structure of their brains, to use mnemonics to remember facts, to reason from classifications, to use perfect practice, how to make accurate inferences, and how to make accurate decisions, but do your youngsters have the skills to implement their decisions? Taking a course in critical thinking does not guarantee they know how to discipline themselves so they can put their learning and decisions into practice. That's why they need some self-management skills.

Key Words:
Cues
Contingency
Using the environment,
Strategies/plan
Self-monitoring and simulation

Q: Why should a contingency be used in some self-management programs?
Q: What are some strategies that can be used in a self-management program?

What is Self-Management?
Key Features:
- Identify where you are (Point A) and identify where you want to go (Point B—your goal).
- Measure where you are (baseline) and how you are progressing.
- Develop a strategy with a plan (steps for the strategy).
- Constantly evaluate your progress. (If you get off track, use problem-solving coping to get back on the right road.)

This is a most important chapter if you are trying to teach your children to become independent learners, to be responsible for their own behavior and wellbeing, to learn techniques that can

122

transfer to other settings that will promote academic performance, productivity, time on-task, and provide them with a sense of ownership and control over their own behavior.

Self-management is a critical skill on the road to critical thinking. Your children must control their impulses, not jump to conclusions, and be able to implement their decisions in an effective manner. Although most of the examples in this chapter refer to academics, these same rules could be applied to self-control goals with personal problems like gaining or losing weight, making friends, improving personal appearance, saying no to drugs, or saving for a special trip.

Self-management uses some of the same steps as problem-solving, coping, and thinking about thinking, with a few added. The primary difference between problem solving and self-management is the *strategies* used. *With self-management your students will be determining the goals, how to pursue them, and their own rewards, not someone else's.* They will decide what personal strategies to use like making a reward dependent on how they follow their plan or using environmental strategies like being around others who display the desirable behavior.

Q: What's the largest difference between problem solving and self-management?

Strategies for Self-Management Plan

When using self-management, your students will be selecting strategies and planning how to use them. Instead of looking for structure or working backward, like with problem solving, they will be using strategies like simulation, cueing, self-monitoring, and contingencies to build their own intervention programs.

Contingencies

A way to increase attention and develop student *motivation* is to use contingencies. When using this technique, you make an *agreement with your youngsters that if they make the desired responses (like doing their work etc.), they will receive what has been promised, like getting to watch television.* Parents do this all the time when they tell their children to eat their green beans before they get dessert. Some make their children do their homework before they go out to play. Many won't let their youngsters go to the movies unless they have cleaned their rooms. Some even have them do their chores before they get an allowance. It happens all the time.

If continued for a long period, some of the things mentioned above become habits for the children, and they do them by themselves without a contingency. Don't most people eat their meals before dessert? (Well, not every kid would prefer green beans before lemon pie.) But some people become motivated to do things in this order. They like doing their homework before talking on the phone (example of self-contingency). They don't want the homework hanging over their heads—it makes them feel a little uneasy. They remove the uneasiness by doing the homework first. That's self-motivation!

Q: What is a contingency? Give an example of using it with your children. The definition is above, so record the definition in your own words and use your own example. You'll feel good if you do this, because it will show you've comprehended the concept of contingency. If you can't give an example of a contingency, read again and then look for an example in the next section. That's using the steps for comprehending.

An example of using contingencies

One time I was a substitute for a mathematics teacher in a fourth-grade classroom. I showed and told the concept that I wanted the children to do and asked them to respond by doing some written problems while I walked around the room observing their progress. When I approached a youngster who had not completed any answers, he said to me, "I don't understand what to do." I looked around the room to see all the other children working away.

The instructions were clearly written, and I thought he might have a reading problem . . . or maybe he was just depending on me to do the explaining for him—that's easier than reading them himself—and thinking! I said to him, "I want you to read the instructions again, and if you can figure out how to do the problems,

I'll give you a quarter." (This was when a quarter was worth more.) His head immediately went down, and he read the material like he was a reading whiz. Like a flash, he worked the first problem correctly and went on to do them all correctly. I had used a contingency—"You read instructions, then correctly complete the problems, and I'll give you a quarter."

Of course, you don't want to go around all the time telling your students, "If you will do this or that I will give you something or let you do this or that." You should want your students to do whatever is assigned because they are motivated to do it. But by using contingencies, students can learn the material and become better learners, which may lead to self-motivation and become habit. But there's even a better way! That is by teaching them how to use their own contingency in self-management.

Using self-contingencies

A contingency in self-management is an agreement with oneself to receive some kind of reward only if one achieves a step toward a goal or reaches the standard one has set. After making a goal commitment, your children should plan to reward themselves on reaching their short-time goals—even if it's just saying nice things to themselves.

Do they really need to reward or punish themselves when they achieve or fail to achieve goals? Shouldn't they be able to decide what their goals are and simply go out and meet them? Sure, they can try, and many succeed. But how many people who make a New Year's resolution actually succeed? Only 8 percent—and some of those have a contingency. So establishing a contingency is likely to help.

Using progress or achievement as a self-reward

You don't always need a contingency as a reward for achieving your goal. In some instances you can use self-satisfaction and feeling of accomplishment plus nice statements to yourself. However, as you reach each step of your goal, you *need to see your results* (look at data objectively to see what you have accomplished). In writing this chapter, as I completed a topic (heading) I felt a sense

of satisfaction and said to myself, "I like that! That will be helpful."
And when the chapter was finished, I said to myself, "It is a good
chapter. (However, sometimes I did not say this, so I worked the
chapter over until I said good things about it.) I learned some things
in doing this." When I think positive things about my work, it
motivates me to do more. However, if self-satisfaction does not
work, try using a contingency.

Q: Describe a self-contingency you have used before.

Simulation

*Simulation is approximating the real thing in a form of covert
practice.* It's like playing a movie of yourself in your mind. You've
heard of flight simulators or driving simulators. These are not the
real thing, but you would never know it when you're sitting in the
simulator seat of a B-52 bomber trying to get off the runway. You
can also simulate what you want to do or what will happen, not by
some technical gadget, but by your thinking, and the results could
help you to perform the act. *Simulating future events increases the
chances that you will carry out the intended action so be careful
what you think about. You don't want to think about failing.
Simulating can be the same as what we often refer to as simply
daydreaming.*

If your students see themselves as studying for an exam, this
increases the chances that they will end up studying for your tests.
But even more importantly, if *your students think about the steps to
their goals*, like taking their books home, opening up their books in
their bedroom at 4:00 PM, telling themselves to try to understand
every sentence, completing summaries, then you would expect that
these activities *will increase the chances that they will end up
studying as you wanted.*

Even simulating upcoming stressful events and how to deal
with them have been shown to improve the coping skills of college
students one week later, and students who simulate studying achieve
higher grades.

Your brain acts as if the simulation is real.

When you ask your children to simulate or rehearse an action, their brains will work just as if they have performed the act. If you ask them to simulate the steps to studying, like taking their books home, opening up their books in their bedrooms, reading, underlining and so on, it activates both cognitive and motor regions of the brain. Nerve endings (synapses) fire in their occipital, parietal and frontal lobes. Here is an example of simulation using basketball:

The late Tennessee's Lady Volunteers' coach, Pat Head-Summit, was one of the most winning basketball coaches in the nation among men's and women's teams. In the waning minutes of a game with North Carolina in which her Lady Volunteers were losing by a considerable amount, she used simulation to turn an important game around. During a timeout she demanded that her players lie on the floor and visualize that they were guarding their opponents and smothering them with effective defense. When Pat Summit demands, she commands, and her players did it. After the timeout, the complexion of the game suddenly changed. The Tennessee players came out with a smothering defense to win the game, go on to an undefeated season, and win a national championship.

You can even have your youngsters *go through exercises in simulation*. You can do this by having them list the steps for straightening up the classroom, doing homework, underlining, highlighting, and taking notes. Then you can have them select a goal (like improved scores) and make a map on paper of the steps they would use to visualize each step of the path to the goal. Then *have them visualize the entire routine*.

Self-monitoring

In earlier chapters, monitoring of student learning has been a priority, especially when using the direct instruction method. In this chapter, we turn monitoring over from the parent or teacher to the *students*. Students will monitor *how they are doing before they start* their programs (called a baseline).Then they will *monitor how they are progressing* toward their goals as they accomplish the steps. And of course, they will monitor the achievement of their goals. If they are not making progress toward their goals, they should ask themselves how well they followed their plans and consider revising their plans.

Assume your students select the goal of making a summary statement after every section of reading assignments in order to improve their grades. When they finish reading their assignments, they simply count the number of summaries they wrote. At the same time, they would want to improve their test scores, so you would have them also record their scores before and after starting their program. Of course, it's a good idea for you to monitor their monitoring. In fact, they'll do better if you monitor them until they understand the value of doing so. For recording such things as being on-or-off task or thinking of positive or negative thoughts, I've had students use a golf counter to keep track of their negative thinking.

Self-monitoring students' plans

Next, have your students develop plans to *use cues to help them to follow those plans*. Have the students paste the steps of their plans on their desks. Here's some example of what a plan might say:

- I will look at the teacher and nothing else; if mind wanders, I will remind myself to pay attention.
- I will paraphrase and put it my notes what the teacher is saying so that I will better understand and improve my grades.
- I agree to call a friend only if I improve my scores over my baseline.
- I will keep a record of my test scores to see how I am doing.
- I will keep a copy of this plan pasted on my desk.
- I will keep a diary evaluating how well I've done and write down ideas on how to improve if I encounter problems.

Monitoring cues and consequence

Cues are signals or signs to behave in a certain way. Let's face it, cues cause us to behave and think in different ways. *A cue can be anything that signals a behavior to occur.* Even thoughts can be cues. You respond to cues all the time, like remembering that today's date is your spouse's birthday. You can see or hear environmental cues, like a clock signaling that you can leave the classroom. Cues can be negative or positive. If thoughts are negative, search for the positive. If environmental cues cause negative behavior or thoughts, avoid them or replace them with positive environmental cues. Have a discussion with your students and encourage them to have cues that encourage. Here are some examples that you could discuss with your students:

Cues that discourage
What was I thinking that discouraged me?
Did someone say something to discourage me?
Did I feel discouraged because of my progress?

Cues that encourage
How much progress have I made—based on objective data?
What kinds of environments encourage me (friends, tutor, or study hall)?
What are the thoughts that motivate me?
Did someone say something to encourage me?

Q: How would you get students to determine what their baseline is for completing their assignments?

Using the Environment to Help with Self-Management

Key Features:
• Arrange environmental conditions so that the desirable behavior is likely to occur. As you know, children influence children and so do parents and teachers. The physical environment does, too. You certainly don't talk as loudly to a friend in church as you do in your car, and you don't drive over the speed limit when you see a police car following you. Your children are influenced by *where* they are, *who* they are with, and what others do. You can use the environment, including people, to help your students reach their goals. Examples

would be studying with people who study or posting their grades at home so parents can see their progress.

What follows are some tips for using the environment:
- Don't tempt them to do something that blocks the attainment of reaching their goals. *Don't put the desired object before them or make them think about the desired item if you don't want them to have it.* Don't you remember when someone received a gift for which you craved deep down and how hard it was to watch that person use the gift? That's shear torture! If you have a youngster who wants to lose weight, don't keep the potato chips on the table. Better yet, don't have potato chips in the house.
- Make the home or study room conducive to studying. You don't want distractions, do you? Certainly not! Have no TV or radio on in the background. Don't have people singing, laughing, and dancing when your children are trying to study. That would not only distract them, but also make the studying seem like punishment.
- Have other students to help. Sit your children near children who study, pay attention, and are otherwise on-task. Also, have the other children encourage any progress your students make. You could even provide a reward for a group who studies together and reaches a shared goal.
- Use a public display of progress. People who make a public display of their progress toward a goal do better than those who do not make their progress public. People who are trying to lose weight lose more when they post how they're doing. Parents especially should see a record of progress.

Environmental cues

Think about cues for a moment. You don't go around smiling and saying hello when no one is around. Seeing someone is the cue to smile and say hello. You can introduce cues for your children to behave in a desirable manner.

Sometimes children forget to follow their plans to reach their goals. One of the easiest and most effective ways to remind

130

youngsters to stay on track is for them to use cues to remind them of their plans or strategies. Some children simply paste their plans on their desks. Others have found that when they paste tags around the house with reminders to do their homework at 6:00 p.m., they are more likely to follow the plans. They can even use their cell phones or other electronic devices to remind them. Such reminders can also be used to think positively about their schoolwork or the work they have accomplished toward goals . . . another way to continue to reinforce themselves toward achievement.

In his book *I Can Make You Confident*, Paul McKenna cites a study where depressed participants were given colored stickers to put around the house, along with instructions to think positive thoughts, using the stickers as cues. In two weeks, neuroimagery showed participants' brain scans moved from that of depressives to happier brains. Make your children happy by reminding them to think happy thoughts!

After teaching your students the strategies for self-management, have them recite the rules (using contingency, detecting and using cues, monitoring, and simulation). Then have them tell you a general rule for using these, like "These are ways to help me become more effective in using self-management, and that will help me adjust to all kinds of problems."

Essence

It's so simple to use the environment in self-management. You should remember how to do this. Notes will do it-even better review the notes every once in a while.

Chapter 11

Learning Self-Management Rules

You've read a great deal about self-management like strategies for selecting a goal and developing a plan. You've also learn how to use the environment in helping you achieve your goals and how visualizations can be used. Now, this chapter puts what you've learned into rules for self-management and it provides several examples of self-management contracts that set the goals, determine how to reach them and how to use a self-contingency. Your children will do this all by themselves.

Key Words
Positive and Negative Aspects
Short- term and long-term goals

Q: What are the rules for self-management?
Q: What are two major aspects of setting a goal to consider?

Rule 1 Evaluate the positive and the negative aspects of seeking a goal

When you discuss the positive and negative features of a goal, you already have a goal in mind. The discussion then is to weigh the benefits and liabilities of using self-management to solve the problem. Have a discussion with your students in which you list the positive and negative aspects of achieving a goal, such as studying at home after school.

The benefits might be making higher grades and feeling smart. The down side of studying at home might be the interruption of playing or talking with friends. Help them see the value of studying by giving them information on what would happen to them in the long term as well as the short term (discuss general reasons). This process is called *comparative reasoning.*

For older children, the discussion could include the merits of a self-management program (like controlling when and how the work will be done, of being one's own boss, and determining one's own reinforcement). Guide your students into seeing the merits of a change, and have your students *summarize the advantages at the end of your discussion. Listed below is an example:*

Positive	Negative
Higher grades	Takes away free time
Feel proud	Tolerate boring subject
Qualify to practice in sport	Interferes with video games
Progress toward graduation	Not being able to talk in study hall
Parent won't fuss at me	Less time on smart phone
Make my own decisions	
I can make my own plan	

Students can even rate how positive or negative each factor is on a scale of 1 to 5 to determine how important each one is, don't just count the number of items in each column. Charles Darwin made a list of advantages and disadvantages of getting married to his cousin. He had three items for marriage and six against. But he settled on marriage. Some factors are more important than others.

When your students decide that there are more positive than negative benefits to self-management, have the youngsters make *commitments* to use self-management. Have them write or say summarizing (general reason) statements like, "There are a lot of reasons for doing well in school. It will open up all kinds of doors like job opportunities, going to college, getting a scholarship, and it will please my parents. I can do it my way not someone else's way, and I will feel competent." (Some children would be more likely to make a commitment to their own personal goal, like developing more friendships, than they would with a goal you suggest.)

Rule 2 Develop a goal

Tutors must keep in mind that they will still be following the problem-solving steps given in the chapter on problem-solving. The problem or goal is the first step. Goals may be long term, such as earning a college degree, or short term, such as doing well on a single exam.

Start with a short-term goal.

Although long-term goals give you direction, *it is the short-term goals that are the steps to getting where you want to go,* and it is the short-term goal with which your children start their journey. They will go inch by inch to make it a cinch.

Never select a goal that a dead man can do.

Don't have a goal of "staying in your seat." A dead man can do that. A graduate student of mine turned in a baseline for a high school student she was working with, showing that he was in his seat all the time and did not cause a disturbance during the 30-minute observation period. The baseline was zero! There was no time out of his seat and not a single disturbance. Did we have the wrong youngster? No, a videotape of the youngster showed that he had been asleep.

Make the goals positive, measurable, and not too high.

The best way to eliminate negative behavior is to replace it with a positive behavior that is *incompatible* with what he is currently doing, like doing the lessons instead of roaming around the classroom. (Students can't do both at the same time.) In selecting a standard for your goal, use the baseline to *set a goal that is enough higher than your baseline to be challenging.* There's also a problem of letting children set a goal that is too high. Youngsters frequently get all excited about achieving their goals; and when they don't achieve them, they are really discouraged. Failure is like punishment. They don't want to do what is punishing again. Make goals that can be seen or heard and measured. Don't set a goal of *improving* performance; instead, set a quantitative goal for what *kind of scores* you will make.

Q: What is the problem of setting goals too high?

Rule 2 Develop a strategy and plan

After selecting a goal, develop a strategy and a plan to get there. The strategy could consist of using contingencies or cues to remind the youngsters of their steps, or students can develop their own strategies. Be creative. By monitoring, they can tell if their methods are working. A good plan typically has several steps. Here you could use any of the strategies described earlier. If you do a simulation, for example, you will need to help your *students visualize the steps* to achieving their goals, not just the goals. Tell them to see themselves taking home their books, have them see the clock for time to study, have them visualize themselves going to their rooms to study, and so on through each step of the way. After doing this step by step, have your students run the steps in their minds from beginning to the end

Whatever strategy is used, students should summarize in their own words the goals and the plans and the reasons for achieving the goals. If summaries are effective for comprehension, they should also be effective for the teaching of self-management. *The summary (general statement) could in effect be the building of a belief—and you know how strong beliefs can be.*

Q: Why is summarizing important after using the self-management steps?

Rule 3 Measure where you are before starting

Show your students how successful they are in getting from Point A to Point B b*y having a baseline with which they can compare their progress and see their gains.* It's like a yardstick or a mark on the wall to see if you've grown. Viewing this information could serve as an important motivator, too.

Using figures or charts are a good way to measure the attainment of a goal or sub-goal. Test scores, if given frequently, are easy to use because parents and teachers have these available and students can be taught to plot their progress. Other measures, like recording time-on-task, will require that the tutor check the accuracy of the recording until it is shown to be reliable. Peers can record such behaviors. Also, by getting a baseline before starting a program, tutors can determine the extent of the problem—sometimes even whether it is a problem. I had teachers ask me to record the off-task behavior of a student; when I also recorded other students in the class, I found that there was no difference.

Rule 4 Selects own reinforcement

As a parent or teacher, you could demonstrate how to select your own reinforcement by giving such examples as calling a friend on the phone or watching a funny television show or DVD *after getting your work completed*. Students can create the reinforcement contingent for accomplishing goals or sub-goals.

We know that students who were asked to write about positive experiences for three consecutive days, three months later, had fewer visits to the health clinic and more positive moods than students who were given an assignment to write on a neutral topic. Then why not have your children think or write positively about their achievements? Give them a chance to stimulate their pleasure centers by reflecting positively about their accomplishments. *Encourage students to use verbal or written statements to reinforce their achievements like these:*

- I'm happy I finished my work and improved my scores.
- A good grade like that makes me feel good!
- Hard work really paid off for me this time.
- Hot dogs! I've increased my score by 20 percent.
- I'm happy I did such a good job!
- I'm glad that's finished.
- I've completed the introduction to my paper and I like it!

Rule 5 Monitor program and change when needed

One of the very best ways to monitor how your students are doing is to look at such data as test scores, problems worked per minute, work samples, probe questions, and even oral answers to questions if records are kept. You want the data to show improvement over the baseline scores.

Monitoring cues (self and environmental) that encourage or discourage

Have your students recall what thoughts and incidents happened to them to see which influenced their progress. For example, did they think discouraging or encouraging thoughts? They can also observe objective data like test scores and relate the scores to improvement or falling behind. They can also ask themselves whether they placed themselves in environments that led to success or failure.

Monitoring the use of steps of self-management

When your children set a goal for improving *academic performance,* they need to make certain that they use the following self-management steps:

Questions about using self-management steps
- Did I make small steps?
- Did I follow the steps of my plan exactly as I had written them?
- Did I use a contingency?
- Did I seek help from the environment in accomplishing my goal?
- Did I praise myself for progress or reward myself using a contingency?

If these questions are not answered affirmatively and the data does not support progress, perhaps they should focus on using some other strategies or steps. If students answer these questions in the affirmative and they also demonstrate progress, have them make *a general statement* like "I can set goals and achieve them by making a plan" or "It's good to take control of what I do."

Noting what did and did not work and making improvement.

In addition to using objective data, one of the most effective ways to monitor the attainment of your goal is to describe *what worked well or not well, what could have been done more effectively,* and *what you are going to do now to maintain* or better the improvement. This technique has been shown to improve student achievement, so this could be added to your self-management contract.

Q: Why would you suppose that teachers who monitor students' self-management programs have students who do better than those students whose programs are not monitored?

Example of a self-contingency contract

What follows is an example of a self-contract using a contingency, describing the goal, the plan, and using the strategies of simulation and self-reinforcing statements.

<u>Long term Goal</u>: I will finish 90% of my assignments in social studies class.

<u>Short term Goal</u>: In two weeks, I will improve from where I am now (52%) to 70%.

Strategy for using rules of comprehension and using the environment to help

- I will bring my pencil and book to class.
- I will sit up and pay attention while listening or reading.
- If I start to think (daydream) about sports, I will pull my ear or pinch myself to remind myself to change my thoughts to my book or teacher.
- I will try to understand every sentence I read.
- If I don't understand, I will read the sentence(s) and underline what is important.
- I will use what I have underlined and use subheadings to guide me in doing an assignment.

Strategy of simulation

- I will use visual imagery (simulation), starting with seeing myself checking that I have a pencil and my book in my backpack when I come to school or with me when I study at home.
- I will see myself looking and listening to my parents or teachers.
- I will see myself reading and rereading sentences I do not understand.

- I will see myself asking my parents or teachers questions when necessary.
- I will see myself checking to see whether I highlighted and summarized a section or page.

Self-Reinforcement (contingency)
- Each day, I will text my girlfriend and tell her I made my goal . . . when I do.
- If I do it every day for a week, I'll take her to a movie on Friday.
- I will note the progress I am making and *say something nice to myself about my achievement.* Also, I will keep a record of my assignments completed.

Figure 8   Recording Assignments Completed

Days

	1	2	3	4	5
Frequency Assignments	4/6	¾	5/6	2/2	1/3
Percent Completed	66%	75%	83%	100%	33%

Example of assignments completed.

Example of starting a self-management plan to eat healthy

Here's an example of the dialogue for forming goals, defining concepts, and utilizing the environment as a self-management program is started:

Nia: Mom, I was talking to Hsian today, and she said she is eating healthy . . . and she looks great! Could you help me to eat healthy? (Making a commitment to a self-management program.)
Mom: What exactly do you mean eating healthy? Eating less red meat? Or fewer sweets? Or not eating as much?
Nia: I don't exactly know which of these to use? I'll look on the internet to see exactly what I would need to do to eat healthy. (Nia looks at *Office of the Department of Disease Prevention and Health Promotion.)*
Nia: Mom, I looked at a US Government website and found a lot of things I could do.
Mom: Alright Nia, you need to set a goal.
Nia: Well my goal is to eat less red meat and consume less sugar.
Mom: You have a goal, but before you develop a plan; let's see how much red meat you eat each week and how much sugar you ingest.
Nia: I already know we eat meat every night. Could you just serve it four times a week?
Mom: That's a good idea. Let's talk to your dad. (Nia finds she drinks three or more soft drinks each day. Now she has a baseline and she is already utilizing the environment by asking her Mom to reduce the meat they eat.)

Rule 7 Coping with failure

Utilize the rule for problem-solving and coping when you have problems with maintaining your progress or are stymied with getting it going. Stick with problem-solving coping, not maladaptive coping, even though the latter may reduce your emotional distress. Have your students ask themselves questions to determine what may have caused their failures. Have them check to see if they followed the basic rules for self-management. Have them determine whether they used the rules for learning a specific subject.

Questions your children should ask themselves about using self-management steps:
• Did I evaluate my strategy and plan to see what may be causing my failure?
• Did I consider using more than one strategy, like using a contingency or cues to remember the rules?
• Did I use positive thoughts when I made or maintained progress?
• Did I praise myself for progress?
• Did I use problem-solving and coping strategies to find the best way to handle an unsolvable problem?

Questions for difficulty in achieving specific school subjects
• Did I refer to the definition or steps to use with process concepts and compare what I did?
• Did I try to understand every sentence I read, rereading when I did not understand, looking for examples, and seeking help?
• Did I do some kind of organizing by putting concepts and sub-concepts in some kind of order?
• Did I underline so I could review the important points? Did I review?
• Did I use mnemonics to master the facts?

A self-management program for daughter

Tonia is having a problem completing an assignment and still having time to do some activities she likes to do. Mother should first have a discussion with her daughter about the merits of getting her homework done and the advantages for doing her work on time. This is done in the form of a contract, but instead of the contract being done between Tonia and her mother, the contract is done by Tonia for Tonia. Tonia sets the goals, the conditions, and the rewards as well as keeping a record on her progress.

Problem

Tonia is given a reading assignment over three chapters in her world history class to be completed over the weekend and will take a test over the material on Monday. However, Tonia has made plans to go to the movies with friends on Saturday night and go for a picnic at the lake on Sunday after church. Tonia will follow the problem-solving rules over her predicament and she must do her own monitoring and select her own consequences. Here's how she does it:

Problem Identification

"Well, I've got a heck of a problem here. Let me see if I can break it down. I must do the assignment and work in the fun things too (problem identification). Not only do I need to do both of these, but I need to really understand that assignment because I have an A in that class and I want to keep it—besides, I like history (problem identification).

Contingency

Studying comes first so I can't go out as I had planned until studying is finished. When I finish, I'll get to go with my friends. Now how much time do I need? About three and a half hours, maybe?

Reinforcement

(The consequences for Tonia are getting to do the things like seeing her friends, going to movies, and watching the basketball game AFTER she did some of her studying.)

Using the environment

"First I need to figure how to do the studying. I'll start right now as I have study hall coming up after this class. No distractions there! (Using the environment.) I could go home and spend at least an hour or two more before Jill comes over to watch TV with me. I'll do that without the radio on (using environmental control). I'll sleep until eight in the morning for a change and spend another hour right after breakfast as mom and dad won't be asking me to help around the house that early (planning). I need to do my laundry and help mom clean up the back porch. I'll set the alarm to get up at eight (Using an environmental cue to get out of bed.)

Personal strategies and plan

"Now I need to 'understand' what I'm reading. I'll try to comprehend every sentence and not get in a hurry. I'll need to make certain that I try to answer some questions even though they are not in the book, like who did what and when . . . and some 'why' and 'what if' questions. I'll write a summary of each topic, as well as underlining (comprehending). I need to organize . . . maybe around dates as I can connect these to American History which I already know . . . or maybe causes (making meaningful and organizing). I'll be careful to make my inferences are based on explicit evidence when possible. Now, I need a half-hour for review on Sunday night. I can work that in *before watching* the Lady Tennessee Volunteers play basketball on TV."

Reasoning

This chapter used *cause-and-effect reasoning* when using data to reason. If your children realize (reason) that by studying with a friend who stays with the studying helps, then your children can reason that this could also help them control their own studying. This is called cause-and-effect reasoning.

After demonstrating with an example of cause-and-effect reasoning, have your students reason the following problem: Assume that your mother is home-schooling you and your three siblings. (That means there are four of you.) All of you are on-task and doing what she tells you to do, but when she goes out of the room, you start to talk, run around the room, and even sing. As soon as all of you hear her coming back into the room, everyone starts to study. You've seen this happen again and again. Now you could use cause-and-effect reasoning to answer the following questions: First, determine the critical feature of cause-and effect reasoning as you did with learning concepts. *Causal events cause a behavior or another event to follow.* You touch a hot stove (causal event). It causes you to remove your hand (a behavior or event).

Q: Did the mother's leaving the room cause the students to stop studying?
Q: What would happen if a parent/teacher did not leave the room?
Q: Did something else happen when the teacher left the room that could have caused the children to quit studying?
Q: How do you know this didn't just happen one time?

Q: How do you know it wasn't Harriett who was the first to jump up, causing the rest of the children to play and sing? (This could be true, but Harriett jumped up because of the teacher left the room, and that caused a chain of behaviors to follow.)

Essence

Write the answers to the questions and you will learn more. Try it with your students, too.

Chapter 12
Learning to Think Critically

Many people think that because they are effective problem solvers or good at comprehending that they are also good critical thinkers. Not so! Of course you need to be effective in problem solving and comprehending in order to be a critical thinker, but there's more to it than these things. You must evaluate the accuracy of the messages you receive as well as the accuracy of your thinking, and then you can apply reasoning. It was mentioned in the first chapter that you likely "prescribed to preposterous beliefs "and are not even aware of it. In this chapter, you see why you do not recognize your beliefs as preposterous. This is the first of six chapters that will allow you to directly teach your children the basic elements of thinking critically. Some chapters include practice activities. You will be using all the skills you learned earlier along with new skills about monitoring and controlling your own thinking.

Key Words:
Humility
Massaging
Framing
Explicit, implicit
Vested interest

Q: What are the steps for being critical of the messages you receive?
Q: How does inductive reasoning work?

What is Critical Thinking?

Everyone does critical thinking; just ask your state and national senators or congressperson. Even ask the president. Ask your city mayor or your city or county counsel representatives. Ask your teachers. Parents want teachers to teach critical thinking. And teachers say they do. Around 75% of teachers say they teach critical thinking, yet only 29% can define what they mean by critical thinking. So now it's time to define critical thinking. There are many, many definitions. The definition used in the next six chapters is that *critical thinking is the use of the very basic skills of learning (like learning concepts, facts, and comprehension) to produce knowledge, being skeptical of your own knowledge as well as others', and then reasoning with this knowledge in an effective manner.*

Value of critical thinking

Surely you want your students to think critically about all the decisions they have ahead of them. If they can think critically without being ruled by habits, pressure, and emotional garbage, all kinds of good things could happen to them. Decisions about using drugs, healthy eating, exercise, and building friendships come early in life. Later decisions like choosing a job or field of study, or how to invest, or issues like global warming, water pollution, population growth or personal problems could be faced with an objective view. And there's no evidence that being a critical thinker is exclusive for those who are educated.

Critical thinking is for you and your children

If you think you are going to make your children debate champions by reading this chapter, you may be disappointed. If you think you are going to convince your spouse or friends to think logically, you likely will be mistaken. This book is not about changing others. It is about improving YOUR thinking so you can be a more effective model for your students. After all, they do learn by hearing you reason and think . . . if you will do it so they can hear. It's even possible that by engaging in critical thinking that can be heard, you might change the opinions of a few of your most stubborn and opinionated friends—but that's not too likely.

You must be an effective critical thinker in order to be an effective teacher of critical thinking. You must know any subject you teach, from math to geography, to be effective. Well, that also means *you must know and use the rules for critical thinking for you to be effective in your teaching of thinking critically.*

If you can't convince others when they are dead wrong in their reasoning, what is critical thinking for? *It's for YOU to discover the best possible answers based on what is known today.* It's not to discover the truths—just what's the best answer today. Some truths keep changing. At one time students in universities were taught that matter could not be created or destroyed. Boy, did we ever miss on that! What about classical physics where we believed that for every cause there was an effect? But along came quantum physics—the study of sub-atomic particles—that describes the uncertainties of our observations. This theory has changed the way scientists look at the world. And now there's *chaos*, the unpredictability of dynamic science. But we can find the best answers and keep an open mind even we find only today's best answers.

Q: Are there any absolute facts in science? If not, what should you strive for?
Q: Why is it important for you to be a critical thinker before you can teach critical thinking to your children?

Overview of the Chapters on Critical Thinking and Reasoning

The following figure gives you an overview of what will be covered in the three chapters on critical thinking and reasoning. For this chapter, *you will be covering monitoring the messages from the messenger and using knowledge to evaluate the messages.*

Figure 9   Four Features of Critical Thinking

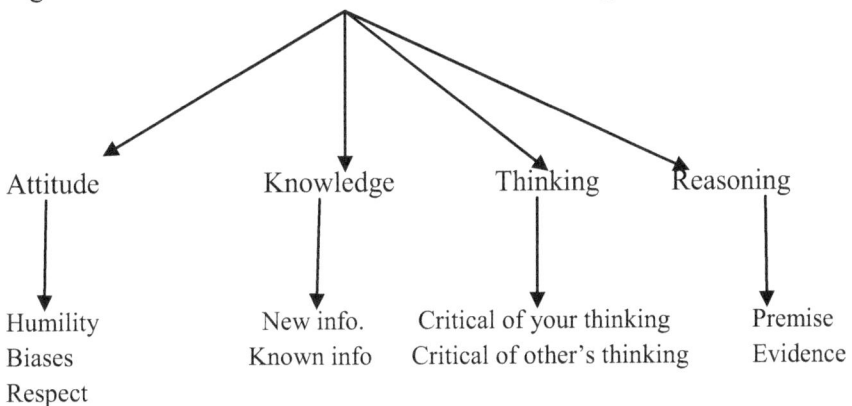

Attitude	Knowledge	Thinking	Reasoning
Humility	New info.	Critical of your thinking	Premise
Biases	Known info	Critical of other's thinking	Evidence
Respect			

Four Components to Critical Thinking

There are four major components to critical thinking. One is "attitude" and it could very well be an indispensable one. The second is "knowledge." You must have something in your brain to work with. The third is "being critical" of what others promote and how *you think*. And last, you must be able to "reason" to be able to understand and organize the information *in a meaningful manner*. All of these will be discussed in the chapters on critical thinking and reasoning.

Be Critical of Messages

As you know by now, critical thinking involves many skills, from defining the critical features of concepts, correcting errors, to problem solving. While most of these help your children to acquire knowledge and reasoning, they must also *be skeptical of the messages they see and hear.* So they are going to learn some new skills that require them to work with their knowledge as they evaluate messages or persuasion, arguments, and predictions. These skills have steps to follow.

Be critical of the message

Steps

Understand the message
What does the message want you to do?
What are the qualifications of the messenger?
What is the evidence for the message?

Using and collecting knowledge

Steps

To clarify the message, ask questions
Use your knowledge to present evidence

Collect more knowledge when needed
"Connect the dots" when evidence is not explicit
Use reasoning

Make certain you understand the problem or message

Parents and teachers, this applies to you as well as your children. Sometimes you can achieve a clear and precise definition of the problem by asking questions of the presenter. But many times you are left to infer exactly what the problem is because some people try to "throw-you-off" in identifying precisely what the problem is. You can use your head and knowledge to obtain a useful understanding of the problem.

For example, assume you hear a speaker on television tell the audience that children who move from one town to another frequently don't do as well in school as those who stay in the same town. You don't know for certain what "don't do as well" means. Could it be scholastically or behaviorally? If you ask for clarification, the speaker may go on to give some evidence that children who move often have more illnesses and lower grades in mathematics and spelling. With this additional information you now could define the problem as: "Children who move from one town to another frequently have more illnesses and don't make grades in mathematics and spelling as high as children who stay in the same town. (It would also be helpful if you could define "frequently.")

Example of being critical of the message of persuasion

The first three features above came from the *Federal Trade Commission, Consumer Information* on the internet. What is the *Federal Trade Commission* trying to tell you? Let me answer that by giving you an example:

Assume you see an ad on television that shows a picture of an Olympic athlete eating a breakfast cereal with the cereal's name flashing in red, white, and blue. You see people cheering in the background and young and old people have smiles on their faces. In her arms is the American flag.

What is the message trying to say to you? It could say:
If you eat the cereal, you can become an Olympian.

What does the message want you to do?
It wants you to buy the cereal.

Who is responsible for the message?
The athlete and/or the breakfast cereal company?

What is the evidence? (added for clarity)
Is this message really true? *What is the evidence* that you will become an Olympian if you buy and eat the cereal? There's no explicit information here. What exactly does it take to become an Olympian? Check on the internet to see what it takes to become an Olympian and you'll find it probably is *natural ability* and lots of *practice* (just like in learning).
Who is responsible for the promotion? Does the athlete have some connection to the cereal company to get her to have a picture eating the cereal? Of course, the cereal company pays the athlete. Parents who are watching ads on television should discuss the four steps listed above as this could be an excellent way to teach your children how to be critical of the message they receive.

Source of information
The source of the information is critical, be it books, newspapers, radio, television, or next-door neighbors. An effective critical thinker also evaluates the context (framing) of the information. Here are some things to look when evaluation the source of the information:
Qualifications:
What are the qualifications of the presenters, and what experience do they have on the subject? Did Billy tell you it isn't dangerous to swing from your feet on the playground swing? Or, did the principal of the school tell you not to?

Vested interest:

You need to determine whether or not the presenter of the information has connections with topics that would cause them to be biased. A scientist who works or receives support from a pharmaceutical company certainly might be biased in evaluating his experimental results.

Reputation for reliable information:

This one would do away with a great deal of TV analysis. These presenters do give you some facts; but sometimes the facts are "cherry-picked" to represent a particular view . . . they are often biased. Most of their comments are conclusions without evidence.

Collaboration:

What about finding out if the information can be validated? In other words, can others get the same results? It's amazing how much information on healthcare makes the headlines but fails to be replicated by other researchers.

Logical:

Does the information make sense? Would any politician develop a health-care plan that would have a "death squad" to determine whether grandmother lives or dies? That would be "death" for the politician. Every claim that appears to be outrageous needs to be reasoned carefully.

Let your children hear you go through an evaluation on the source of the information and then guide them in doing the same thing.

Asking Questions to Evaluate Evidence and Source

If you hear a presenter in person, you can clarify a great deal of the message by asking questions.

Parent/Teacher
Makes presentation
You have just heard a presentation on trips to the moon and back for 100 million dollars. A private company is sponsoring a trip that will make one loop of the moon and bring you back for a two-and-a-half-

day trip. You must pay two years in advance and be over 21 years old and have a doctor's certificate that you are in good health. The trip will take off from Florida in a Russian Soyuz built rocket. There will be room for nine passengers.

<u>Children</u>
Students now ask questions. The examples below are questions they might ask:

- How often has your company made trips around the moon without people?
- How many attempts has your company made to get your rockets off the launch pad without success?
- Who design the space craft and what are their qualifications?
- How well had the Soyuz rocket performed on missions to the space station?
- Has this mission been approve by NASA?

Ask additional questions.

Conclude by asking your students to give the reason for asking questions and getting clarification. Also ask them to state a general rule like "I can learn more by asking questions in a respectful manner that clarify what others mean." Give feedback and make corrections.

Using Your Knowledge

Key Features:
- Use the information you already know to help with critical thinking.
- Seek additional information.

Knowledge is what's stored in your head—all those facts, concepts, principles, rules, beliefs, and experiences. Just like with problem solving, you go right to your brain to look for information to do critical thinking. You should not solely depend on the information someone has given to you to do critical thinking. You should also use what you already know about the issue and contrast, evaluate, and scrutinize both sets of information.

Here's an example you can read to your children of how a youngster might use his knowledge to solve the message about eating breakfast cereal:

Well, let me see what the athlete *wants me to believe*. I should use an inference here, like I learned in my courses on language literature. Since she says, "Eating this cereal gives me a fast start out of the starting blocks," I would infer s*he wants me to believe* that the eating of cereal makes me run faster, although she didn't exactly say that. Since I also know a lot about concepts, and how to look at their critical differences, I can see there is a difference between "getting a fast start out of the starting blocks" and winning a race, and I also know she's talking about herself and not me . . . although she wants me to infer that it will happen to me. Now *I also know* from reading *Track and Field Magazine* that it takes some natural characteristics to do well in some sports. Not many men under 5' 6" play professional (or college) basketball, and not many males weighting under 125 pounds play high school football. I also read how hard sprinters like Wanda Rudolph practiced to become Olympians. By inference, *the message is* for me to buy the cereal. I'm not going to do it because I know it's not likely to help me run faster.

Example of obtaining more knowledge

After hearing this example on teaching elementary school age children how to seek new knowledge, your children can answer the questions at the end of this section.

Child: Mom, should we eat more carrots? Mr. Hamilton, our next-door neighbor, says eating carrots will improve how well we see.
Mom: (Looking for evidence.) Well, let's see. To find out if this is correct or not, I need to look for evidence. Watch me as I look on the internet to see what the *Mayo Clinic* says. Most of the time what they say is based on research by scientists. (Qualifications of the presenter) Here . . . it says that carrots contain antioxidants that help maintain healthy eyes. Now . . . it may be good for eye health, but it

doesn't exactly say that it will improve your vision. It says, "maintain healthy eyes." Let me see if some research has been done on improving vision. Listen, here's one from *Scientific American* saying that a study showed that eating cooked carrots for six weeks helped bring night vision up to normal . . . but that was with women deficient in vitamin A. So Mr. Hamilton is partly right. Eating carrots will improve the night vision of women who are low in vitamin A but not everyone.

Have your children answer the questions below after reading this example:

- What is the message? (That's also considered to be the problem.)
- What does Mr. Hamilton want you to believe?
- Who is responsible for the message, and what are his qualifications?
- Describe how you went about finding additional information.
- Describe where other information could be found.

Have your students make a general statement about following the four rules for evaluating messages, like "If I understand the message and what the message wants me to believe, as well as who is responsible for the message, I can think more critically about the message."

Connect the Dots

Critical thinking is not just recalling the facts or explicit information. Sometimes you must figure out what is happening with only bits of implicit information. You'll need to piece together what is happening. This is called making an *inference* and was covered in the chapter on comprehension. This is often called "connecting-the-dots." Here's an example of making an inference:

Assume you see a young lady dressed in an athletic suit, the latest running shoes, and a ball cap, running down the street. What might your inference be? (The problem)

Evidence	Inference	Conclusion
Running	Exercising	
Dressed for running	Exercising	Lady is exercising

Although you have some information in your head which you should use (like this is the way many people dress when they exercise, and it's not unusual to run for exercise) you still need to make an inference about her intent. She could have been running from someone for all you know. Making inferences is a step in reasoning and will be covered more fully in the chapter on reasoning.

Inductive Reasoning

There's also a type of reasoning called *inductive reasoning*. This form of reasoning is *reaching a conclusion that may be probable, based on the evidence.* It uses inferences as part of the reasoning. Here's an example of a reference to doing inductive reasoning from Charles Dickens' book *Great Expectations*, which was published as a weekly from 1860 to 1861:

"They took up several obviously wrong people, and they ran their heads against wrong ideas, and persisted in trying to fit the circumstances to the ideas, instead of trying to extract ideas from the circumstances."

In other words, they had ideas about who committed the crime, and tried to fit the evidence to them instead of looking at the evidence and see if it fit any of the accused. Here's an example:

Assume that you know that whoever robbed the house took 125 dollars and stopped long enough during the robbery to drink a full bottle of wine, leave a handkerchief with the initials JGK, and was tall enough to reach the wine bottle on the top shelf in the kitchen. This is your evidence. So you immediately arrest 5 people who appear to be somewhat drunk. One of those has a long arrest record, and the others have only minor offences. Now you think (premise) that the long-arrest guy is the likely suspect. Now you connect the evidence to your hypothesis. He's tall enough to reach the wine bottle, and according to his arrest record he likes wine to drink (more evidence). He has over 125 dollars in his pocket. But he does not have the initials of JGK. So you say maybe he left the handkerchief to throw people off—after all, why would a thief leave his handkerchief with his initials on it at the crime scene? (This is massaging the information so it fits your hypothesis.)

With inductive logic you also look at the evidence and see where it leads you. Of the five men, four are tall enough to reach the wine, but only two had 125 dollars, and of the two only one had the initials of JGK. Therefore, you would be inclined *to think* that the one with the initials JGK was *likely* the thief. (When using inductive reasoning, one can only conclude what is *likely*.)

Q: Explain what is meant by inductive reasoning.

Inductive reasoning gives likely conclusions

With inference, you try to put the pieces or clues together to make sense of what is happening. That's very important because many children will be faced with information from classic literature to newspaper reports that they must comprehend by making inferences. In such cases, they will need to "connect the dots" by using implicit information, like you are seeing two boys in a heated argument, watching the boys go outdoors, then hearing banging, bumping, grunts, and falling sounds. Other than hearing the argument and the sounds, that's all the information you have. It's valuable information because it helps to you build an inference that a fight has taken place . . . but you did not see a fight. So don't say the premise is that they had a fight and look for evidence to prove that— although you could do that. Instead, consider looking at the evidence first and see where it leads you, then you can say it is *likely* that the boys had a fight.

Inductive reasoning is a very popular method of reasoning so you'll hear more about it in the following chapters.

Time for Your Children to Practice

After you have demonstrated and discussed the steps for being critical of information, it is now time for your children to practice being critical. Here are a couple of situations (elementary, middle school, and high school levels) that you can have your children evaluate using the four steps described earlier:

- Persuasion:

Ginger is good for an upset stomach. If you take it daily you'll never have stomach problems. Look for the very finest ginger, *Gold Kili*.

- Arguments:

<u>Mom</u>: According to the *Alzheimer's Association* you need to be active, have a healthy diet, social relationships, and cognitive challenges like word-games in order to have a healthy mind.
<u>Dad</u>: Just exercise and don't smoke. Those two things are the most important, according to the research I've read. There's no research evidence that diet and word games can prevent Alzheimer's disease.

- Prediction:

What will be the change in the world's temperature three years from now? (You can use what experts say, intuition, data, or a combination of all three to make your prediction. You need to rely mainly on evidence and sources of evidence on this one.)

You can use the examples above to make your own practice activities.

Essence

This is an import chapter. Be certain to list the steps for critical thinking from the *Federal Trade Commission, Consumer Information* listed on the internet. They are important.

Chapter 13
Learning About Obstacles to Critical Thinking

There are more obstacles than you can ever imagine to thinking critically. You need to be aware of these obstacles if you are to become an effective thinker. Some of these influences are so powerful that you can be told exactly how you were subjected to distorted thinking and you still believe the memories are true.

Q: What exactly is meant by massaging the information?
Q; What are the steps for helping to control your emotions?

Key Features:
- Jumping to conclusions (caused by brain habits)
- Massaging information
- Being framed
- Recalling the gist (recalling the main idea)
- Embellishing (memories get larger or smaller)
- Tunnel vision (not seeing things that are there)

Obstacles to thinking critically

You and your children have some obstacles built into your brain that cause you difficulty in accurately recalling experiences and facts that you have learned earlier; in addition, you have obstacles that keep you from accurately processing new information. Both of these present problems in being a critical thinker.

Figure 10   Problems with Accurately Recalling Information
                           Types of obstacles

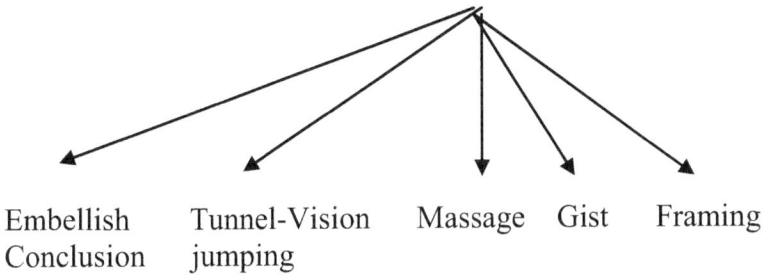

Embellish   Tunnel-Vision   Massage   Gist   Framing
Conclusion   jumping

Jumping to conclusions

Reaching a conclusion is part of critical thinking. You should count the number of times you jump to conclusions! You'd be surprised how often you and your children do it. I find that I jump to conclusions several times each week . . . sometimes several times a day. Most of the time, my conclusions are correct so I don't think much about it . . . err . . . I *think* they are correct. But sometimes they are wrong, and sometimes it's embarrassing.

You know that you have habits that you use all the time without thinking. You walk from the car to the front door while thinking about what happened today at school or work. You don't think of putting one foot before the other. It's a habit to do this. You turn the door knob without saying to yourself, "Turn the knob to the left." You do it without thinking. It's a habit. Well your brain works the same way. You already have a habit of saying that one plus one makes two. You don't have to think about it. But sometimes you need to think before you jump to a conclusion.

Brain habits

One of the major obstacles to critical thinking is that *your brain is already wired to go with the "thinking habits" you already have.* How you thought yesterday is how you'll think today and likely in the future. You may have patterns of thinking that you learned from your parents and the people with whom you associate. Such habits may be honesty, faithfulness, independence, sharing, cooperation, following laws, and on and on. You've learned what is politically correct from parents and community, and you learn religious values in the same way. You've seldom been forced to examine any of these thoughts in a critical way.

Every day, your brain is wired and strengthened in these beliefs. Because you think this way all the time, these thoughts become automatic without much contemplation about the implications of your thinking. Your brain acts just like the reflexive knee-jerk, kicking into high gear with thoughts that are now habit. These thinking habits are a great inhibitor to critical thinking, even though you might reach the same conclusion with a critical examination of these issues. The big problem here is that once you select an answer to an issue, the more difficult it is to change it.

Q: Explain why your brain jumps to conclusions so easily.

Massaging information

Let's assume that you are forced to listen to a television station that you do not like because it presents information you don't agree with. But your spouse forces you to listen to the station and you hear some information that conflicts with what you believe, even though there is some strong evidence presented. When you get contradictory information, your brain has a "fit." (No joke!) It does not like conflicting information and the stronger the information, the more your brain reacts. The amygdale increases in activity as the ventral striatum (section of the brain that anticipates rewards) decreases.

Since this is very unpleasant, your brain wants to relieve itself of this conflicting information. This is done by what is called "massaging" the information until it makes sense to you. Psychologists used to call this *massaging of information*, an adjustment or coping mechanism like using "sour grapes" (saying it wasn't any good anyway when you don't get what you want). When you find a way to make the information more palatable, you make your brain happy again. You have reinforced your brain (made it happy), which increases the chances that you will do this trick of massaging the information again. This is also called motivated reasoning.

Example of massaging the information

Assume you find out by national news that your favorite politician has been sending tax payer money to his business. He has been found guilty of ethics standards. That's quite a shock to your brain so you say to yourself, "All those politicians do that all the time. He's no worse he the rest of those crocks. Besides he votes for what I like." (Now you feel better.)

Here's another example, assume you receive a request for money from a local Catholic Church to feed the poor during the depression. You know they have been feeding the poor and needy for over 50 years. But you say "I don't trust them because they are known to help migrants. They may also spend that money for holy water. I think I'll save my money for some sure way to help the poor." (By saying that, you feel better.)

We all do this almost every day. When I got home from the grocery store the other day, I had a cup of coffee and a cookie and thought about how people massage information. I had been trying to lose a little weight as I have a weight standard that I try to keep. When I decided to eat the cookie I recalled that I had said to myself, "I exercised a lot this week and have eaten well. So a cookie won't hurt." That made me happy. But the fact is the cookie is 50 calories, and that can add 50 calories to my daily intake. I had manipulated the situation so I didn't feel guilty, and my brain was reinforced for doing this.

It's a rare person who doesn't try to fit unexpected information into the mind so it makes sense. At one time scientists believed that animals and plants that existed in their time had always existed and changed little over time. When someone found the large tooth and tusk of a mastodon, the scientists believed these bones to be that of a large elephant. But they noticed that the tooth of the new discovery had a tooth that was cusped, not flat on top like an elephant.

Now they had to fit this discordant information into something that made sense. The best answer they could devise was to describe the difference as just an "aberration" of an elephant's tooth. This made them feel better because this fit into their current belief. They couldn't believe that the bone had come from a creature

161

that had become extinct by some environmental calamity. It took many years before scientists had enough information to make an "inference" that there was once a different set of plants and animals that had become extinct because of some climatic event.

Human beings are pretty much a species of biased creatures. And here's the problem: when you are informed that you are wrong in your conclusions and furnished with conflicting information, you massage it so it does fit, and you become more biased than ever that you were "right" in the first place. Fortunately, your children are not so set in their opinions and beliefs that they will ignore quality information. That's why you stand a good chance to make your children critical thinkers.

Q: Think of something that happened today that caused you to massage the information.

Watch out and don't be framed!

You've probably seen a hundred movies where the police arrest someone who then cries, "I've been framed." If you haven't seen it in the movies, you've surely seen it on the television news or read in the newspaper where someone accused of a crime yells to high heaven that he was "set up" and that he didn't do it. It's often against the law to frame someone; yet most of us are framed quite often by the television news we watch, what we hear, and what we see. Framing means contriving the *context* of information.

Several states now have approved ending of life support. That is, states will allow a medical doctor to assist those whose life is terminal in ending his or her own life. When a survey was conducted, it was found that most people approved of this if described as "end of life support" but they showed less approval if the message was described as "assisted suicide." The same thing is true for describing health care: if it is labeled as Obama Care, more people disapprove than if labeled as the *Affordable Health Care Act*. You've been framed in answering the question depending on how it is labeled.

Recalling the gist

When you go about solving problems, you retrieve information already stored in your brain. But you will likely receive the information as the "gist" of what has been learned. *The gist is different from the essence.* The essence is the most important feature(s) while *the gist is a general idea*, like recalling that something costs a dollar instead of the actual cost of 97 cents. In other words, when you recall the gist, you have the general idea. That's important!

Professor Elizabeth Loftis' research shows how memory distortion can happen to most of us in problem solving. You may have seen accidents where people get hurt. You've probably seen car wrecks and plenty of pictures of bombings on the news. Time and time again, in movies, you've seen people get injured. Keep in mind the picture of what happens when people get injured by an accident as you read about Loftis' study.

At a high school football game, one of the players was injured from a head trauma and was knocked unconscious. The injury was so severe that an ambulance was called to take the player to the hospital. Years later when those who attended the game were asked to describe what had happened; a great number of them described the player as bleeding from the injury, which was not the case. Now think about what you know when someone is injured by an accident. Many, many of the cases involve bleeding, so you have stored these in your memory, just like those who saw the accident described above. With time, the people recalling this incident must *have recalled the gist of having an injury (if you are injured, you bleed)* instead of the accurate facts. So memory in problem solving may also be faulty when using past information to solve a problem. Time can also distort or embellish your memory.

Q: What's the difference between the essence and the gist?

Embellishing information

Embellishment is adding information to enhance something when it may not be accurate. Many storytellers add details to make their stories more interesting . . . so do politicians. You may do the same thing when you try to recall a memory. Garrison Keillor, speaking on *National Public Radio*, told a story of embellishment about a man who had a brother in the same town in which each were very friendly and would often walk into each other's homes unannounced. That caused no problem for the families, as they were close and felt at home in each other's homes. One day the sister-in-law went down to the basement to do some laundry. While she was there, she decided to add the robe she was wearing to the washer; however, that left her with only her underclothes on.

In the meantime her brother-in-law had come into the house. Finding no one home, he sauntered into the kitchen. As he was making a peanut butter sandwich, his sister-in-law came up from the basement and on opening the basement door, she and her brother-in-law were both in a state of shock as they peered at each other. The brother apologized and made for the hall door.

Through the years, the brother-in-law's picture in his mind of his brother's wife, in her underclothes, grew to that of the most beautiful figure one could ever imagine. His mind had distorted his memory to make it more exciting. This story describes (with a few changes) how our mind can embellish some of our memories.

Not seeing things that are there

Perhaps you recall having a discussion with someone where you became a little heated and under stress in some way. Later in the day you may recall the incident and wished that you had remembered to remind the other party of several factors of importance to support your views. Why didn't you think of them during your discussion? If this discussion distressed you, it probably narrowed your perceptional field—or gave you 'tunnel vision'. You were concentrating so much on one aspect of the discussion that other thoughts were blocked out. Hours later when you relaxed, you recalled what wasn't *available* to you during the discussion.

In his book *How We Decide*, Jonah Lehrer cites studies in which participants who were stressed were asked to note when they saw a blinking light in their peripheral field. The researcher found that those *participants who were stressed were twice as likely not to see the blinking lights as a control group*. Their *perceptual fields* had been narrowed, thus their abilities to solve problems diminished. Of course, if you don't recognize something, there's no way to recall what is not recorded. So that tells you to try to relax when you perform critical thinking.

You don't need to be emotionally upset in order to have tunnel vision. David DiSalvo describes a study were participants were asked to count the number of times a basketball was passed while watching video. While participants were counting, a woman dressed as a gorilla slowly walked across the back of the screen, paused to beat the costume's chest, and slowly walked out of sight. Half of the participants did not see the gorilla because they were so focused on counting.

False memories

You may think that your memories are perfect, but your thinking is false. You have all kinds of false memories. Like Mark Twain once said, "When I was younger I could remember anything, whether it happened or not." He readily realized that his memories could be false and could lead to big trouble for thinking critically. Elizabeth Loftis found that she could implant false memory into people so they would recall being in places they had never been and of meeting people there that never existed. This is not a rare occasion; according to an article published in *Memory* and reviewed in the *Monitor on Psychology*, about one-third of a study's participants recalled false memories like taking hot air balloon rides and playing pranks on others—and they could remember the details.

Example of being critical of your thinking

When you think critically you evaluate a problem, decision, or someone's statement (or contention). Let's assume someone was charged for bank robbery, and you must testify that he did the robbery. You need evidence that he robbed the bank. Assume you have some explicit evidence: you saw him pull out his gun, tells the cashier to "fill the bag with money," and saw him take the money and leave out the front door where he was apprehended by a police officer. You have a great deal of evidence for a conviction as a robber and it is explicit—you saw it.

So in doing critical thinking you want to examine the evidence, and there was plenty of it in this example; but let's change one thing: assume that you did not see the man apprehended at the door. He was caught three weeks later and still later you must now identify the man. You saw him; seeing him was explicit information. However, you have just read in this chapter how your recall can be affected by recalling the gist, or framing (what was said to you before examining the lineup), and how much your memory embellished or minimized the identification and whether you massaged the information. As you probably know, witnesses are not too accurate in their identification of possible criminals. So you may not be able to accurately identify the man in a lineup.

You Are in Control

This is important! This is about how you control what is put in your brain and where it is recorded. You are in control of your thinking. Because you put information (whatever you see, hear, read, or feel) into different parts of your brain and because you then must retrieve of the information when you recall it by putting the pieces together, you and no one else is responsible for what you recall (or believe to have happened). For example, if you see a street beggar asking for money for a meal and you see a young lady give the man five dollars, you might say, "What a naïve young lady she is for you know there are several social organizations in town that will provide food to the hungry." On the other hand, you might say to yourself, "What a thoughtful and kind young woman she is to give the beggar five dollars when there are social organizations in town that provide food to the hungry." If you perceive the situation to be one of naiveté, the information will go to several parts of the brain related to this, and if you see the situation to be an act of kindness and thoughtfulness, it will be recorded into different parts of the brain. What you record is what you will recall!

Why do people have different perceptions of the same thing? It's because of all the experience in watching movies, hearing parents and family and friends discuss similar situations as well as culture and religious differences. All these experiences are recorded, and the more often they are recorded, the stronger the neural pathways become so you may recall things faster and more vividly. (Recall that neurons that fire together, wire together.) There are other factors that may influence how you place information in your brain and whether you accurately recall memories. Memory (or knowledge) is one of the most important aspects of critical thinking. You must be careful how you record information in your brain because when you recall it, it may or may not be accurate.

Essence

Don't forget to list the essence of the chapter. You can do it by bullets so it's to the point and easy to understand. Notice that I'm fading out my prompts to get you to list the essence of the chapter and answer questions.

Chapter 14
Learning Rules to Think Critically

Now you're going to learn how to use your head! In the previous chapters, you've seen some obstacles to thinking critically, so it's time for you to learn how to teach your children how to overcome these brain obstacles. You do this by teaching them to have an objective and open attitudes toward the messages they are receiving, to stop biases from distorting messages, to control their emotions, to monitor their thinking so they will inspect every obstacle, and to use the steps for critical thinking to overcome these impediments. There are practice activities for your children in this chapter.

Key words:
Implications
Open attitude
Alternative explanations
Emotions

Q: What are some methods for changing attitude?
Q: What are some methods for controlling emotions so they will not interfere with your thinking?

Attitude Helps to Overcome Obstacles to Thinking

In the last chapter, you were told of several obstacles to critical thinking (like recalling the gist, embellishing or minimizing information, and framing). Now you are going to be given some steps to help overcome these obstacles.

Attitude is critical to your thinking and the thinking of your students. *Your attitude is what you use to evaluate your perception of) your world, including yourself.* You may see the cup as half empty or half full. Are you willing to learn or do you already know it all? Your mind is open or your mind is closed on some topics. *But for critical thinking, it is your attitude about being open to different information that makes an important difference.* If your attitude is "closed" on a topic, you won't listen to new information, and as a result you are going to have a difficult time being an effective critical thinker. Your attitude would include humility, respect, your biases, an understanding of the positions of others, and being open to other experiences.

Humility (I don't know)

To be humble you put yourself in a position of saying, "I don't know," and this may make someone seem smarter or better than you. But it's to your advantage to say, "I don't know." After all, critical thinking should be for you. You should want to know the most probable correct answer to questions. It would be to your advantage.

Most people don't want to say, "I don't know," because it smacks at their self-concepts. You must accept the fact that you don't know everything and be willing to continue to learn more about our world. You've missed a great opportunity to learn something because you've closed your mind to the issue. (An open mind should be demonstrated by you for your children. Let them hear you say you don't know, and then let them know that's the way you are going to learn something new.)

Q: How could you let your children know that you don't know it all?

Recognize that you are biased

Being biased is judging information based on your pre-existing beliefs . . . and you better face it: you are biased because of your culture and the people you are around, like your parents. Most people vote like their parents, they develop health habits like their parents, and they select a religion based on that of their parents. It is not just parents who determine your bias; it is also the people you are around, your friends, neighbors, workers, and the part of the country where you live. This determines what programs you listen to on the radio or television because your friends, doctors, and employers determine what station you listen to (they have them on when you go to their homes or offices).

Your biases are so subtle that you don't even realize you have them, even though they affect your behavior. When judges' rulings dealing with women were investigated, it was found that when they became the father or mother of a daughter, their rulings became more favorable for women's rights than before their daughters were born. You can bet that they never recognized it!

Young children generally don't have a great deal of emotion attached to their biases and only develop this with age, so starting to explain biases while they are young may open their thinking to other outcomes. (When you discuss issues, add a statement recognizing that you could be biased, so your children can hear your thinking and recognize that a different answer is possible.)

Here's an example of how being biased can work:

Assume you are the district attorney of a large city and one of your detectives presents a case to you and asks you to prosecute the person. As you should, you ask for evidence against the person. He shows you a video of a nicely dressed 60-year-old woman examining an expensive item and walking out of the store with it in hand. The outside video shows her walking to her car, putting the item in the backseat along with some other items and driving off. The house detective stops her before she leaves the parking lot and takes a picture through the car window of the item in the back seat. Should the district attorney bring charges of shoplifting?

Is there sufficient evidence? You reflect just about two seconds before saying, "We'll press charges . . . and by the way, what is her name?" Make certain you put yourself in the position of the district attorney when you find out the lady is your mother. Will you have second thoughts? Will you want to examine the video again? Will you carefully look at other things going on in the store? Would you have reviewed the video if you did not recognize the woman? Would you review the video only after you discovered the woman was your mother? You very likely would be biased in what you would do when you found that the thief was your mother.

Respect

Don't laugh or roll your eyes at a wild idea because there is probably some reasoning behind what you heard or saw. (Especially don't let your children see you do this.) If you're going to learn, you must stay open to the ideas of others. We all make conclusions using the information we have. And most people have different information. By questioning, you can find out the information others use to make their conclusions. It's just possible that they know something you don't know. Here's an example of how a wild idea was considered crazy or impossible and a wild idea about the future:

- Almost everyone said the Wright brothers were "crazy" to try to fly like a bird.
- According to Yuval Harari, in his book *Homo Deus*, humans will become immortal, living forever. (A project sponsored by Google is currently underway to prove this.)

Let's assume that you were living in 1907, and you read in the newspapers about some brothers who say they are perfecting a flying machine. They have been flying kites for years and now believe they know how to control these so that men can fly a machine. You think about all the stupid ways men have tried to fly: Jumping out of barn lofts flapping man-made wings, being shot from cannons, and when the Smithsonian paid for an engine-power glider that crashed into the sea without flying more than three seconds. You conclude that those brothers are crazy.

A man named Glenn Curtiss read about the Wright brothers. Intrigued, he visited them to learn more about their "harebrained" idea of flying. He listened to them tell how they had succeeded in flying attached to a kite. They said they could fly if only they could control the man-flying kite, and they said they were going to try to control the aircraft the same way birds control their wings—not by flapping but by tilting their wings to land and change directions. Curtiss didn't think they were crazy. He didn't laugh; he tried to understand what they were saying. He went home and developed his own flying machine, thanks in part to listening and trying to understand what the brothers had told him.

Your students need to listen to others: let others talk. Because, among other things, brain imagery found that people get a brain kick (boost in activity in the brain's reward pathway) when talking about themselves (and their ideas). That's also a good way to show respect by listening and to making friends at the same time.

Emotions

Emotions are big blockers to critical thinking . . . maybe not big, but *giant* blockers! Certainly emotions "stamp the event into memory," but emotions can also work havoc on your thinking. Think about it; haven't you ever been tongue-tied when upset, trying to think straight. You don't hear what the other person says, and you can't remember what you should say (until you calm down). Your mind is just blank for a moment. (I've had students forget their names (momentarily) when called on unexpectedly.) Emotions are going to throw your thinking back like a reflex where you jump to conclusions and get more upset at discordant information that does not fit your beliefs.

If you really want to be a critical thinker, you must prepare yourself to use the rules mentioned above before you put yourself in a position not to get emotionally upset. When you're overcharged on a bill, don't attack, but prepare yourself to hear what the explanation is, be humble, try to understand what they are saying, and do this with compassion as if they have some reason for the outrageous cost they expect you to pay. And remember, you are biased. Being emotional has been shown to make you less empathetic, less compassionate, and less able to see someone else's view, according to Stanford neurobiologist Robert Sapolsky. Being compassionate, empathetic, and open to new information are essential to critical thinking.

The key here is to be set, ready, prepared to do this. Be a critical thinker. Be set to ask questions to help you understand where they are coming from. If you ask the right question, you might get them to see the fallacy of their thinking . . . but don't count on it. And, of course, you might find the fallacy of your own thinking . . .

that's what you want if you want to be a critical thinker. Delay reacting because it sometimes takes as many as 20 minutes to cool down.

You can control your emotions. According to Bruce E. Compas, Jennifer K. Connor-Smith, Heidi Saltzman, Alexandra Harding Thomsen, and Martha E. Wadsworth, who wrote in the *Psychological Bulletin*, "coping responses involve efforts, often under a person's control, to manage thoughts, emotions, and behavior that accompany a stressful experience." So let's look at some ways to control your emotions.

Steps to teaching your children to control their emotions

Frustration happens when you are blocked from achieving some goal or are threatened in some way. Your heart rate increases, blood pressure rises, your blood vessels constrict, and your muscles tighten, all of which block your reasoning. There are several ways to handle this:

Reframe the situation

Reframe means to express the situation or concept in a different way. You can teach your children to visualize being calm, hold their tempers, and not jump to conclusions by using the same techniques (steps) that were described in the chapter on self-management. Now physicians in training are using reframing to cope with the death of a patient. Instead of seeing themselves as healers, they are taught to see themselves as someone to keep the patient comfortable and help the relatives through the worst days. Another example of reframing was mentioned in *TIME Magazine* in January 2017. The article explains that students who were told that having stress about taking an exam is a "good" thing outperformed students who were told nothing of the sort.

Be set to be open to information

Teach your students to have the correct attitudes for being open to new information, that they should respect others whose ideas seem farfetched, and that their beliefs can bias them. Teach them not to fear mistakes, but to recognize mistakes as feedback that help them do better next time. That's a way of reframing.

Emotional and problem-solving coping

Emotional or problem-solving coping have been found to be effective. Use the techniques covered in the chapters on problem-solving coping to better control your emotions, like identifying what steps you may have missed or identifying the events that stress you. When students are blocked from achieving their goals, here are some self-statements they can use to help them cope:

Questions students should ask themselves:
- What did I do wrong? (problem-solving coping)
- Let me go back to the directions to see if I understood.
- Let me compare what I did with the definition or with the steps.
- I could check with my book or a reference book or ask someone for help.

Adjusting to the problem that cannot be solved
- I can see there's no way to solve this, so I should figure out the best way to live with it (emotional coping morphs into problem-solving). Since I can't solve this problem, let me think of a plan to live with it (make the best of it).
- I'll think of something positive (thought switching).
- What thoughts relax me?
- What situations that upset me should I avoid?
- What thoughts upset me, and I how should I avoid them?

Summarize with general-reason statements. (Problem-solving is the most effective way to face problems.)

Sleep on it

Your grandmother may have told you that when you are upset and want to "fire away" at whatever is causing you distress, "have a good night's sleep on it instead." Seems like grandmother knew that before the psychologists, but now they have found that sleep does, in fact, reduce stress and anxiety—factors that inhibit critical thinking and making sound judgments. Sleep causes you to moderate your emotional experiences. It flattens out both good and bad experiences. In one experiment participants had an emotional experience and were kept awake while another group was allowed to sleep. The participants with no sleep had much more vided recall of the emotional event then those who were allowed to sleep.

President Harry Truman would become very angry at his opponents and write them hostile letters, but before he mailed them, he slept and changed his mind. He never mailed a letter . . . except one when his daughter was criticized for her piano recital. If you can't sleep on it, pause a few minutes before responding.

Self-Monitoring

When you self-monitor, you talk to yourself, tell yourself what to do, and questioning yourself whether you are doing what you are supposed to be doing. You do this by asking such questions as: Did I do that right? Could that be wrong? What exactly was I supposed to do? Did I do it? I'm trying to understand every sentence. I'm going back and rereading this section so I can understand it. I'm looking for an example. I made a mistake so I'll compare what I did to the concept definition. I'm organizing by making a map of the concepts. I'm using the rules for practice by reviewing everything at the end. If I start to think about something besides achieving my goal, I need to remind myself to be on-task.

Now with critical thinking you need to monitor your thinking about collecting information and the source of the information. You say to yourself, "I know what he wants me to believe, but there is no evidence." You may ask, "Did I recall the gist? Let me think about that." Or you might say to yourself, "Did I use what explicit information there was before making an inference?" And you should be certain to monitor your attitude by asking yourself such things as, "Did I really try to understand what he was saying? Could I have asked more questions?"

Be Critical about What You've Read in this Book

Do you really believe everything you've read in this book or is it just a bunch of "stuff" that an old retired professor has dreamed up because he didn't have anything else to do? And do you believe in what you've read enough to teach your youngsters some of the skills? Or could you actually use what has been presented so far to help you evaluate the questions above in a critical manner? If you can, you are on your way to becoming a critical thinker.

Let's apply the rules given to you in the last chapter that were suggested by *the Federal Trade Commission, Consumer Information.*

• What does the message want you to believe? (There are different skills to critical thinking and they can be taught.)
• What does the message want you to do? (Teach your children the skills to critical thinking.)
• What are the qualifications of the messenger? (Use the internet to look for publications on learning and behavior modification under the author's name.)
• What kind of evidence is there for the message? (Examine the research in the appendix showing there are several skills to critical thinking and that critical thinking or intelligent thinking can be taught.)

Rules for Critical Thinking

So far you should have learned how to evaluate messages you receive by examining the evidence for the message and the qualifications of the messenger; Of course, you should make certain that the terms (concepts) of the message are clear. You should ask questions if needed to determine the meaning of the terms and the evidence if not given. Then you should determine *what you do* with the message. That's where you examine the obstacles for clear critical thinking covered in the last chapter. Here are some rules to help you make certain that you do not distort the message:

Rule 1 Examine your attitude by believing you could be wrong.

Everyone is biased, even the best critical thinker, but they recognize it and try to consider it in reaching a conclusion. Also respect what others are saying even if it seems outrageous. The next chapters provide more information on being open to information.

Rule 2 Try to control your emotions by reframing.

Try a positive explanation to something negative by reframing or give it another title. And of course, you could use problem-solving coping to see how you might analyze the message you are evaluating and live with it if not solvable. And don't forget that sleeping on it really helps to settle you down.

Rule 3 Self-monitoring

Make certain that you use the rules just mentioned to help you accurately evaluate the message. You can ask yourself question like "Did I recall the gist?" or "Did I ask enough questions to clarify the problem?" or "I know I'm biased but did this influence my conclusion?"

Essence

Some important things have been said in this chapter. You can extend your memory by writing the key features.

Chapter 15
Learning to be Open-Minded

This chapter will be an "eye-opening" chapter for most of you. You will learn the difference between open and close-minded individuals and how this is related to your youngsters' intelligent thinking. You will also learn how effective and infective individuals predict the future and what exactly do effective thinkers do to make performance effective. Since you will know how to be an effective thinker, you will also learn the techniques to teach this to your youngsters.

Q: What exactly do you do to be open-minded?
Q: If you teach children in a group to be open-minded what attributes would you want the group to have?

Key Words:
Be open to new information.
Seek new information.
Be able to change conclusion in the light of new information.
Use data.

Being open to information is just one of the major steps to critical thinking, but a very important one. According to this book, open minded means recognizing you are biased, recognizing you can be wrong, being willing to change your belief in the light of new conflicting information, doing this in a respectful manner, and seeking new information if needed.

Note that this definition requires you to be *active* in weighing new information. It also must include that you are willing to search for additional information if needed and not quickly jump to a conclusion. If you take a test on thinking critically, you are given scenarios and expected to make decisions on the information given; but in the real world, you may need to seek more information in order to make a meaningful decision.

Now there is research that can determine how accepting you are of new information and how willing you are to modify your beliefs in light of the new information.

Tests that measure open mindedness

In 2013, Uiel Haran, Ilans Ritov, & Barbara A. Mellers published a study in which they determined if people who are open minded could predict uncertain qualities (like winners of football games) more accurately than closed-minded individuals. Here are *two* of the questions on their test. These serve as examples of being open or closed minded. Questions were answered on a 7-point scale:

Open minded: People should revise their beliefs in response to new information or evidence.
Close minded: Changing your mind is a sign of weakness.

Keep in mind what is meant by being open and closed minded while you read the remainder of this book.
In a study by Kruglanski & Webster (1996), using a 5-point scale, participants were simply asked which sentence accurately described them. These questions accurately predicted intelligent thinking.

- I am one who prefers to know one big thing.
- I am one who prefers to know many small things and am content to improvise explanations and evaluate on a case-by case basis.

Predicting real life events

If there are several skills necessary for you to think critically, perhaps each of those could be measured to see exactly how much each of them contribute to accurate decisions, like predicting world affairs. And if there are several skills, could using *all* of them result in even more accurate predictions than using only one or two? This appears to be the case. But how do we measure accurate predictions? Most critical thinking tests measure logic and problem solving and are based on scenarios of arguments, persuasions, and predictions. Making predictions is a most difficult and important task if you consider making predictions on financial and world affairs. These are important as many world affairs have a direct influence on your welfare and the welfare of your children and grandchildren.

Here's how a study by Barbara Mellers and associates from the University of Pennsylvania and Missouri, published in 2015, tested whether open-minded individuals can make more accurate predictions than closed-minded individuals about geopolitical events. They had 743 participants make 150,000 forecasts on 199 events over a 2-year period. All participants took a test of knowledge of world events, an intelligence test, and a test of *Active Open Thinking*. Here are two examples of the items the participants attempted to predict:

- Whether North Korea would test a nuclear device between January 9, 2012 and April 2012?
- Will Moody's downgrade the sovereign debt rating of Greece between Oct 3, 2011 and November 30, 2011?

Participants were given the questions and could make a prediction anytime within the timeframe they wished. They could, if they wished, search for more information and make as many revisions in their initial forecasts as they desired. The time required to make a decision was recorded.

Results of the research

It should come as no surprise to you that *knowledge* of world affairs was related to accuracy of predictions. (As you've been told, you can't reason on an empty brain.) The same was true for intelligence, but the influence of intelligence diminished the second year of the study, which is consistent with the finding on emotional intelligence *where perseverance increases over intelligence as a predictor of grades.*

It is important to note that individuals who scored high on the *Active Open-Minded* test also scored high on accurate predictions. What follows is a *contrast* of what open-minded thinkers did compared to close-minded thinkers on several studies.

180

Attributes of active open-minded thinkers:
- Reflective
- Weighed new evidence against favorite belief
- Spend sufficient time on a problem
- Considered others' opinion
- Updated evidence for or against belief
- Need for cognition (organizing, elaborating, and evaluating)

Attributes of closed-minded thinkers
- Jumped to conclusions
- Did not consider alternatives
- Focused on first answers
- Ambiguous evidence in favor of initial conclusion

Can Open Mindedness be Taught?

The answer is simply YES. Open mindedness can be taught.
- Participants who received training in what I will call data-based reasoning made more accurate predictions than those without the training.
- Participants who took part in group discussions where forecasts were discussed and evaluated made more accurate predictions than those without the group discussion.

   The bottom line is that most accurate predictions were *not* made by individuals having a single intelligent skill. Instead, the most accurate predictions were made by those who had several skills. These skills consisted of combining such variables as political knowledge, intelligence, less need for closure, fixable thinking, deliberation time, and belief updating. And the good news is that intelligent thinking can be improved by lessons on *data-based reasoning* and group activities where rationale for predictions can be presented, evaluated by all members, and updated if desired.

How to overcome biases

As was said many times before, it is difficult to overcome your biases, let alone even realize you are biased. First, let's look at what causes you to be biased in the first place. There are probably many causes for this, but let's look at *your clan* (the people you associate with) and how they impact how your brain works. Your clan may be your family or neighbors, your church or work associates, your school chums, social media groups, or a combination. The ones who have the most influence on you are the ones you hold in highest esteem.

When you meet with your clan, they tell you their thoughts (or stories, some of which may not be true) about their values of teaching children to use condoms, the need for meat inspectors, climate change, capital punishment, assisted dying, and their concerns about the national debt. Some of these issues they may feel very strongly about, so keep in mind that *emotions stamp the event into memory* (both negatively and positively).

. Because of language, your brain allows your clan to paint a picture of the future and speculate on cause and effect occurrences records the events described *like you really experienced them.* Since and you hear them again and again and you like it because it stimulated your pleasure centers—making you want to hear more and more. According to Leo Widrich's writing in *Buffer Social*, by simply telling a story (that may or may not be true) we can plant ideas, thoughts, and emotions into listeners' brains. And by telling them again and again, the neural pathways become stronger and stronger.

How do you change your biases in the light of all this continued reinforcement you receive from your clan? There's one simple way that has been shown to help some youngsters; change the clan. Studies have shown that when students go off to college and meet a new clan, by the time they are seniors, they have significantly changed their beliefs about some issues.

Group work with a different clan may change your children's critical thinking and biases. *But a change will not happen unless your new clan can objectively evaluate information using similar steps as mentioned in evaluating messages of persuasion.*

Story telling

According to Yuval Noah Harari, author of the book *Sapiens: A Brief History of Humankind,* sometime between 30,000 and 70,000 years ago a mutation changed the brain of *Homo sapiens* in a manner that allowed them to think and speak in an unprecedented manner. *Humans* were now able to *connect a small number of sounds to produce an infinite number of sentences,* giving them the opportunity to communicate more precisely about their world and experiences. Instead of making a sound to alarm the clan of a nearby lion, an individual could now tell exactly where the lion was, how to avoid him or attack him, and even how to cook him.

Language helped *Humans* communicate how to coordinate their actions and thus they became more socialized. Their language not only described their world more precisely, but they were now able to invent fiction, including such imaginary creatures that were part man and part animal. They invented fictional stories and games, moral codes, ghosts, spirits within objects (rocks, trees, streams, fish, birds, animals) and religious rituals. They invented all kinds of abstract concepts that do not exist, like the modern abstract concept of "limited liability." *The ability to speak about fiction was one the most unique aspect of this change in language.*

Since *Humans* had the ability to invent fiction, they now heard and invented new and wonderful conspiracy stories, not based on facts, but on implicit information. These stories can be so compelling and interesting that *Humans* simply ignore the facts. *Humans* seem to have a powerful "disease of astonishment." Stacy Schiff says, "Our attitude for the miraculous endures; we want to there to be something just beyond our ken. We hope to locate the secrete power we didn't know we had . . . ."

Now we no longer communicate with our clan around the fireplace. But now we have electronic communication that allows us to reach thousands with the click of a button. And what power-grabbing stories are lies made up without any evidence? We now hear plenty of these. How can we tell that these are really lies when the person telling the story sounds so sincere, and the stories strike an emotion? If we believed in witches not too long ago, why not believe in more lies? Now there are other ways of thinking, like with false news and alternative facts. Our storytelling is no longer a family affair but has been taken over by electrically transmitted information, especially through social media. The content of the information transmitted to us has also changed from communicating family values, facts, and moral fiction, to telling alternative facts and false news which may sound much more appealing than the cold facts. False news travels six times faster than true ones on twitter

Q: Is a conspiracy theory appealing to people? How can this be overcome?

Take fake news seriously

Fake news may be a more serious problem than you may have realized. Alan Miller, founder of the nonpartisan *News Literacy Project,* refers to the amount of misinformation "equivalent of a public health crisis." Here are some reasons why: Many people don't critically read the social media material before passing it on. You can't be an effective critical thinking without at least reading and trying to comprehend the message.

You've got to be on your toes on social media messages according to TIMES' Katy Steinmetz because false stories get tweeted six times as fast as true ones and two-thirds of Americans get news from social media. So you're going to get plenty. To help overcome false information, use the basic rules for being critical of messages describe in earlier chapters. Also use a fact checker. And be award of "Deep Fake" video. They look real.

Using groups to teach critical thinking

Keep in mind that a group of peers can be a clan. And stories are told and retold by clans. If properly arranged, new clans can be formed to allow students to evolve through information beyond what was transmitted through their original clans. One of the most often used methods to do this is group discussion. Before you start, remind your students to use an attitude that will overcome the impediments to critical thinking—like being close minded. You can post the components of an open attitude on the blackboard, their smart phones, or make a poster of what comprises a positive attitude before you start your group work. Here's why group work helps to teach critical thinking using problems or scenarios:

- Children will see how others keep open attitudes.
- Children will see how others use evidence to reach conclusions and how factual data is preferred over opinions or conspiracy theories.
- Children will see how others monitor their own thinking.
- Children will see how others change conclusions in the light of new evidence and reasoning.
- Children will be exposed to group norms which have an influence on adopting the group norm.

Steps for Being Open-Minded

You use a number of skills in critical thinking like knowledge, defining concepts, comprehending, problem solving, coping, and so on. Critical thinking has some additional skills that are often difficult to master, but you can do it. These skills along with the skills already covered, provide you with some rules for thinking critically. What follows are the rules for being open-minded along with more examples and some practice scenarios.

Rule 1 Monitor your thoughts (your work and your knowledge)

Students should do a great deal of self-monitoring as they go about the early skills of learning. They monitor as they are trying to understand every sentence they read, they monitor if they reread something they don't understand, they monitor if they compare their answers to the definitions or examples when correcting errors, they monitor whether or not they follow the steps for problem-solving and for self-management. (Self-monitoring goes on in most of the steps to critical thinking.) In addition, they should be very critical of messages and messengers. Now they must also monitor whether *their thinking* is influenced by how they retrieve what they have learned from memory.

As you now know, what you see and hear is placed in your mind as you match or associate it to information already stored. If it doesn't fit, you fix it so that it does. Because you do this, you need to be extra critical of your own thinking—not just the messages you receive from your environment—but what you do with it.

You also can inspect your thinking after you have reached a conclusion and scrutinize some of the pitfalls listed below:

- Consider whether you are using the *gist* of the information.
- Consider whether you might have missed some information because you were focusing on other aspects. (You had *tunnel vision*.)
- Consider whether the information was *framed* to bias you toward a conclusion.
- Consider whether you have *embellished* or minimized the information.
- Consider whether you jumped to a *conclusion*.
- Consider whether you *massaged* the information.

Rule 2 Have an open attitude

Here's where all the items mentioned above about scrutinizing your thinking come in: Your students (and you) must *recognize that they can be wrong*. They must be patient enough to *listen to all the information*, not just what they believe in. *They must recognize that they are biased and that they jump to conclusions all the time.* Here are some questions you can ask your students to help them understand they can be wrong (some are correct):

- Have you ever believed someone (maybe like your brother or sister) took something that belonged to you and later you learned you were wrong?) Discuss this. (All of us have, so you see that you can be wrong; therefore, listen to others and listen hard, because they may be correct . . . or they may be wrong.)
- Have you ever missed an item on a test that you thought you had answered correctly?
- Do you need oxygen to breathe? (Yes)
- How high can elephants jump? (They cannot jump.)

186

- Is the magnetic pole located in the north of the earth? (Yes, but it has switched to the south.)
- How long can a cockroach live without a head? 9 seconds. 9 minutes, or 9 days. (Ans: 9 days)
- Who invented the electric light? (Federick de Moleyns, Joseph Swan, and J. W. Starr invented the electric light. (Thomas Edison perfected it so it would burn longer.)
- There is enough water in Lake Superior to cover North and South Americas in how much liquid? O, 1 inch, 1 foot, or1 yard. (Ans: 1 foot)

Recognizing your biases

It's not easy to recognize that you are biased. The judges, who became more liberal in their ruling, didn't realize it; and the description of the district attorney (above) whose mother was charged with shoplifting didn't recognize he was biased when he asked for additional information. He probably attempted to massage the information when he saw it was his mother by saying to himself: "She probably didn't realize that she had not paid for the item."

Understanding someone else's view

Remember, it's almost impossible to understand someone who has a different view if the issue is loaded with emotion. It's an *incredible rarity, but it can be done if you have the backbone to do it.* Take for example a topic that you have made up your mind on like increasing the number of refugees to this country, food stamps for the poor, or abortions. If you are against it, write a paper pointing out the advantages of doing it. If you are for it, write a paper on pointing out the advantages of not doing it. You must have a list of exactly ten items. This has been done with students in debate classes. It has been found that many change their minds after being forced to defend the opposite of what they believe . . . but they do it for a grade and most people can't have such a powerful contingency. Nonetheless, you should try to understand the presenter's view.

Rule 3 Using data to monitor open-mindedness

Recall how important data was to problem solving, self-management, and objectively monitoring how students are doing, like what caused a youngster to not complete homework or finding the patterning or structure of numbers. People who are taught to use data learn to be more accurate in making predictions (that's critical thinking) than those who do not receive the training . . . so it's important. Since you now have some idea of how to tell whether people are open-minded, you can now collect some *data on how you are doing in teaching* your children to be open-minded. The following questions might give you some ideas for measuring how well your students are learning and are open to information that may be different than their beliefs. This test can be given before you start your teaching on how to be open and again after you complete the teaching:

• When you make up your mind about something, do you want to stick to it no matter what?
• When you are told you are wrong, do you try to convince the person who corrected you that you are right?
• Are you a person who will listen and try to figure out what someone with crazy ideas means?
• Are you a person who quickly points out what is wrong with someone's crazy ideas?
• When you do not agree with someone, do you ask him questions to try to understand their thinking?
• When you do not agree with someone, do you try to end the conservation as soon as possible or try to convince her she is wrong?
• Are you a person who takes time to decide on issues and is willing to obtain more information?

These are just examples that can be used to measure open thinking, which is an integral skill in critical thinking. You can collect data on the above questions by adding their scores before and after your teaching and use it as a measure of how much your children learn. Such questions also make excellent discussion questions. (You can modify the questions for different age groups.)

Rule 4 Reaching a conclusion

Many of the key features are the same as when using problem solving, but with critical thinking you must *consider the implications of your conclusion* and whether you have followed the steps in making a decision that *considers how you think*. When you reach a conclusion, you are looking at the claims or problem, examining the information that supports the claim, examining your own inferences and biases, and then reaching a decision. This is probably one of the most important aspects of critical thinking because it may cause you to behave in a way that influences others . . . like your students.

If you conclude that the claims that have been set forward in this book are likely true, then you may incorporate them in your program. That may cause your students to become more effective thinkers and that in turn may influence your students as they decide to use drugs or not, drag race, work or go to college, buy a home, secure a financial future, and even look both ways before crossing the street. Or maybe it won't have any effect at all. Look at the evidence: implicit or explicit, source and message, before making a conclusion!

Essence

There are two important factors in this chapter: One, you should know what a new clan is. Also remember that a discussion group should use objective data and the steps for teaching open-mindedness. Review your notes and you will remember a lot more.

Chapter 16
Learning to Think Critically and to Reason

So you've collected all the evidence, looked at the qualifications of the presenter, and monitored your thinking to ensure that your brain habits will not distort your information. Now you must be ready to do some reasoning with the information. You've looked at messages of persuasion, but there are other kinds of messages, like reasoning from truths and arguments that require different kinds of reasoning. In this chapter, you'll find a number of different types of reasoning and practice activities that you can use with your children.

Key Words:
Premise
Minor premise
Conclusion
Messages

Q: What do you do when you've been given a premise or message that you do not think is correct?
Q: What are the steps to monitor your attitude?

Reasoning

Reasoning is a skill just like that of comprehending. You need it in order to be an effective critical thinker. There are many types of reasoning as described earlier. Some of these can be taught at a preschool level, like reasoning by elimination; others are more sophisticated, like cause-and-effect analysis. The type of reasoning you use would depend on the problem. If you are trying to determine what causes a chemical reaction, you might use cause and effect reasoning; if you were trying to find the missing element, you might want to use elimination reasoning; if you are trying to make a decision, you might use comparative reasoning by listing to the advantages and disadvantages of your options.

Figure 11   Steps to Reasoning

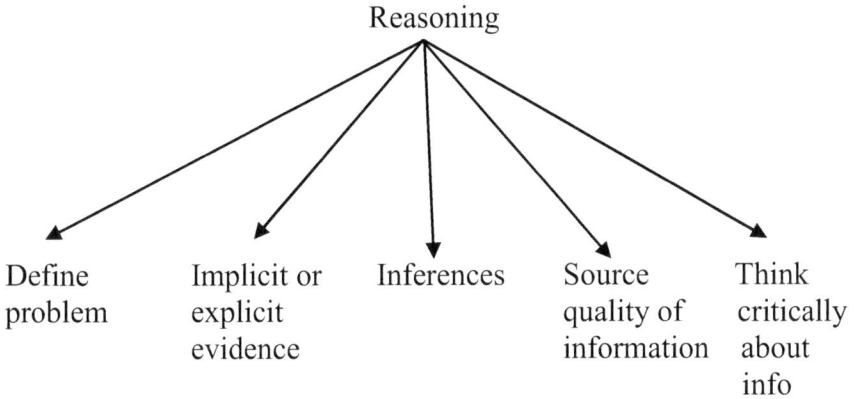

Reasoning

| Define problem | Implicit or explicit evidence | Inferences | Source quality of information | Think critically about info |

Reasoning means thinking in a logical manner in order to form a conclusion. The factors above should be considered when your students use reasoning.

Deductive reasoning

Deductive reasoning starts with a premise (*what one says is true*). Then a secondary premise is given that, if true, means that a conclusion must also be true. You've heard many times about the deductive logic on being mortal:

All men are mortal,
Socrates is a man
Therefore Socrates is mortal.

Deductive logic is most often used with science and mathematics. The reason? These fields mainly deal with scientific facts that have been proven to be factual. (Actually they are the best answers we have at this time, and they are useful in solving more problems based on these facts.) The same is true for mathematics. Here's an example of deductive reasoning with mathematics.

If 3X = 9
And if 1Y = 1
Then 3X+ 1Y = 10

There is an old saying that you might take to be true: "Ladies should be first." You open the door for them, take their orders first, and serve their food first at restaurants. So here's an example of the reasoning for Shana going first:

Ladies go first (premise that is *absolutely true*—at least for this example.)
Shana is a lady (secondary premise is true)
Shana should go first (conclusion)

In deductive logic, the premise is always considered to be true. Here are some examples with this type of reasoning. Try these with your children:

• Dad says I should not ride my bike in the street when learning how to ride because it can be dangerous.
I want to ride my bike in the street.
Therefore it would be _____.
• My teacher says it hurts all children who are bullied.
I am a child.
Therefore bullying would hurt _____.
• All lambs have wool as white as snow.
Mary has a lamb.
Therefore Mary's lamb has _____.
• All men's cells have a membrane.
Billy is a man.
Therefore all the cells in Billy's big toe _____.

Q: What are the steps for deductive reasoning when you believe the premise is true?

Premises that are not accurate

Your youngsters should be vigilant as to the accuracy of the premise. Usually the only absolutely accurate premises come from mathematics and science. Here are some questions to give them on how to spot inaccurate from accurate premises:

- Girls who are smart can obtain good jobs when they grow up. Marilyn is smart; therefore she is likely to:
- Men who are kind and nice to others can be cheated all the time. Chuck is nice. Therefore, it is likely that:
- All men are mortal, Josh is a man, and therefore it is likely Josh is:
- Ordinary men are smarter than the president. My dad is ordinary. Therefore:
- Boys like to wear perfume. My brother is a boy. Therefore he likely likes:

Looking for evidence that a premise that is true

You should not take it for granted that the premise is true. Here's a message from your friend and another message from your teacher that describe an argument. One says smoking is not harmful and the other says it is harmful. Have your students look for evidence that smoking is or is not healthy in the following example. Be certain to define what is meant by "healthy."

Your girlfriend, age 13, has been offering you a cigarette every school day for the past four days when the two of you have lunch off campus together. She tells you it is fun to act like the high school kids and not to worry about getting addicted. She says she has been doing this for more than a month now, and she can stop smoking anytime she wants.

On the other hand, your health teacher also told you that smoking one cigarette will not addict you, but mentally you may like what you are doing (acting like high school kids) and it will become a habit; therefore, you will continue to smoke until you have enough nicotine in your system to become addicted. Your health book also says that half of the people who begin smoking before age 20 eventually die of smoke related diseases, and you will develop big wrinkles under your eyes at an early age. Now what are you going to do? (Be certain to consider the source of the information and even look up more information from the internet or books.) Demonstrate or have your students determine the following:

- First state the premise (What does the teacher and friend wants you to believe and do?)
- State the evidence for the premise
- State the qualifications of the person giving the evidence
- Make a conclusion as to the accuracy of the premise

Although evidence is given, you can fact-check online to see how accurate these statements are. Using deductive reasoning as to how it would work:

Premise: Smoking is not harmful to people—according to friend.
Secondary Premise: You qualify as "people."
Conclusion: If you agree that the premise is true, if follows that you could smoke without being harmed. (But was there evidence that the premise was absolutely true? No!)

Demonstrating how to evaluate the source of information

The source of the information was covered in the first chapter on critical thinking, but you can use this material for a demonstration or as a practice item. Your students' questions should focus on the source's qualifications as an expert, whether the source has a vested interest, if the information is reliable, if it is collaborated, and finally if it is logical. Here's an example of your dialogue when you teach (demonstrate) your students to evaluate the sources of information:

I'm going to read this article from the *Monitor on Psychology* and try to understand what the persons who wrote the article are saying, and since I can't ask questions, I'll need to try to reason if what they said is correct.

Preschoolers appear to learn math best when they're taught using brightly colored or unusually textured objects that are unfamiliar to them, according to research conducted by psychologists at the University of Notre Dame. In two experiments 133 3-year olds were randomly assigned to the counting tasks that used different types of objects. The researchers found that the perceptually rich objects—such as sparkly pom-pom or neon pinwheels—helped capture the children's attention and helped them stay focused on the mathematical task . . . ."

Alright, let me see if I understand what the authors are getting at. It seems they are saying that if bright, unusual objects are used to teach preschool children mathematical tasks, they will 'learn best' (paraphrasing the presentation). The *problem* would be to determine whether the claim that preschool children learn best with brightly colored and unfamiliar objects is supported by evidence. Let me think a minute . . . maybe I could have a different problem? No. (This is coping.) So the writers give some *evidence* citing that 133 children were used in the study and that number included a control group. (I must admit that I like studies that use a control group . . . but I'll be careful not to let that influence me too much.) The authors didn't say how much more the children with the bright objects learned than the control group.

The *qualifications of the researchers* were high. This was published in the *Journal of Child Development*, and was conducted by faculty at the *University of Notre Dame*, which makes the source acceptable . . . now there's evidence, but the authors *may want us to make a conclusion* before giving the evidence that the study "appears" to help the children learn. Perhaps they want the reader to make a conclusion that "better learning occurs when bright, unfamiliar objects are used for teaching counting tasks." But the authors say preschoolers appear to learn . . . the word *appear* does not sound that strong . . . so that's what I'd say as my *conclusion* . . . it appears to help learning based on this one study. *Long-term implications* are . . . we don't know if the gains will be retained, but I assume it will do no damage to the children. Since you would probably agree that the qualifications of the presenter are high, here's how this could be reasoned:

Premise: Bright-colored objects help children to learn math more effectively.
Secondary Premise: Colored cars and trains are colored objects.
Conclusion: (If the premised is true, the secondary premise would be true. But there was not absolute truth to the premise because the word "appears" was used. With inductive reasoning, this would have been "likely" true.)

Inductive reasoning (using inferences)

When you don't have explicit information (you did not see, hear, or feel the event) you will likely use some form of inductive logic like with the example of the house or building being on fire. Making inferences is an important skill you need to use to think critically. *An inference is coming to some kind of conclusion based on your past experience and the information given to you when the information is not explicit (you don't directly see it).* It can be based on some implicit information and some inferences. For example, if you hear the siren of an emergency vehicle and you smell smoke, you might infer that there is a fire someplace. That is, you make a conclusion that there is a fire someplace. You make this inference because you have learned that emergency vehicles, like fire trucks, go to where the smoke is. But you have no explicit information of a house or building being on fire. The sound was explicit evidence and so was the smell of smoke, but you did not directly see a house or building on fire.

You do this all the time. Here's how it works: First you have a premise, and evidence for the premise that is not explicit, then you have an inference about the information, and last you draw a conclusion.

196

Premise and evidence ——————→ (Inferences) ——————→ Conclusion(s)

Inferences are very helpful to your thinking. Just like the example of the fire and smoke, you make sense of things without implicit information, and most of the time you are correct. But sometimes you may be hampered by making inferences.

Example of using inferences

In 2014 a lady went to court claiming that a gas company had caused her health problems. She had no problems until she moved to a farm close to a gas company that practiced fracking. Soon after moving she broke out in a red rash and severe illness. When the doctors could not find any physical cause for the illness, they suggested that she look for environmental causes. She found out that a neighbor had kept a record of the gas-related accidents like spills and leaks. She then connected these incidences to the times she had been in the emergency room for service. (Her emergency room visits corresponded with the fracking incidents. The case went to a jury.)

Fracking causes illness (claim or premise) ——→ Evidence ——→
Record of spills (data)
Record of emergency visits (data)
Doctors suggested environment.
Inference (based on experience, evidence, or research)——→
Conclusion: Spills *likely* cause illness.

No one directly observed the leaks and the illness occurring together. No one found any changes in her blood work or skeletal makeup. But most people would make an inference that the two are related based on the evidence. The jury made the same inferences and found the gas company guilty. But their inference may have been influenced by their biases and past information. (In demonstrating reasoning like this, you can make a chart like the one above to show how you reason, collect evidence, and how you reach a conclusion.)

Q: What do you say about conclusions with inductive logic?

Example of demonstrating self-monitoring with inferences

In this example of making inferences, you will monitor your attitude and critical thinking steps. Inferences have been taught in the chapter on comprehension. To work through this example, you will put together many of the steps you learned earlier. Demonstrate how you make an inference by using the scenario below:

Parent/ teacher:

Alright, I'll start with a story about a policeman. I'll try not to be biased one way or another about police. I read good and bad stories about them all the time, and I have a friend who was a policeman. I'll try to not let that influence me. What I need to do here is use the rules for critical thinking as I go along. Children, you need to see whether or not I use them!

Assume that a policeman on patrol is passing a bank and hears the burglar alarm go off. He sees a man dressed in a suit, carrying a briefcase, running from the bank get into his car and speed off. Now I need to define the problem. The burglar alarm would suggest a bank robbery and the man running would suggest that he might be the robber trying to get away (inference).

Did I do that correctly? I don't want to just jump to a conclusion. Could there be another explanation? The policeman hasn't received a call on his radio that there is a bank robbery in progress . . . (information). Maybe it could be a medical emergency . . . but it's the burglar alarm that is going off (evidence). Why would the alarm sound for a medical issue? I'm looking at the information here: the man is running, has a briefcase, drives off rapidly, and the burglar alarm is going off . . . this make me want to make an inference that this man may be a burglar, although no one saw him commit the robbery and the policeman did not receive a call. Should he wait for a call?

No (conclusion). Therefore, does he need to pursue the man (behavior)?

Ask yourself these questions:

Did I let my biases influence my thinking? No, I'll think about that. I do like policemen in our town.

Did I define the problem? How? The policeman had to make a decision as to whether to pursue the man running from the bank. Did I consider multiple explanations? What were they? (Maybe the man was running to get away from the robbers and his briefcase has money that he was going to deposit.)

Did I collect information on both possibilities? Since I can't ask questions, I know only what the scenario describes.

Did I make an inference? What was it? First, I made an inference that the running man was a robber, but I thought of some other explanations.

Did the inference make sense? How? Yes, there was some information used to make an inference. The man running and carrying a briefcase are given, but there is some conflicting information; the way he was dressed (in a suit) made me think he was running away from the robbers because he didn't want them to get whatever was in the briefcase.

Did I reach a conclusion? What was it? It wouldn't hurt to go after him.

Did I monitor my thinking? How do I know? I kept asking myself if I were framed, did I jump to a conclusion, had I massaged the information, recalled the gist, or embellished the information.

Did the conclusion influence my behavior? Yes, I decided that the policeman should go after him.

What, if any, long term consequences could there be to my decision? Maybe I made a mistake and the robber was still in the bank.

Here's a diagram of the critical thinking sequence:

Premise: Bank is being robbed.

Evidence	Inference
Burglar alarm	signals burglar
Man running	robbers run
Has a briefcase	briefcases contain money
Drive away fast	trying to get away

Conclusion: Could be a robber

After you have finished with other examples, *have your children state the value and dangers of inferences. Then have them state a general reason or belief like, "Inferences are very important, but one must be careful when reaching a conclusion on inferences alone without explicit information, because they can sometimes be wrong.*" Also have them comment on the value of using several steps to critical thinking to reach a conclusion.

Predictions

You certainly can predict what will happen if you put your hand on a red-hot stove, but some things are more difficult to predict. You can use deductive logic to predict some things, even though you cannot see the future, but you must also use inferences to predict the future. Past experience can be used to help you make inferences. Let's examine this example of predicting the weather:

Here's a simple example of reasons (premise) and conclusions:

Channel 10 weather reports that according to all their models, it will likely rain today.

Statement (premise): Rain is likely today.

Evidence: All models indicate likely rain (how accurate are these models?).

Conclusion: Rain likely

Since you believe the evidence is valid and reliable (based on your personal experiences) and it is from a respected source, you conclude it will likely rain.

Reaching (minor premises) other conclusions based on accepting the first conclusion

Reason (models predict)⟶ Conclusion 1 (likely rain)⟶ Conclusion 2 (better take umbrella)

So you could go on and reach several conclusions based on the evidence from Channel 10. You might want to take the car with the best window wipers or wear a raincoat. Both would be drawn from the information from Channel 10. (You can help your children use this kind of reasoning by giving simple examples like the one on weather or demonstrate this with everyday events that they read about or see or hear on television, digital devices, and radio.)

Example of quality of evidence

When you use reasoning, you are trying to find the accuracy of the premise and evidence. (Remember, a premise is something believed to be true.) You do this by determining the accuracy of the evidence (plus your bias and past knowledge and experience). If someone tells you that it is going to be extra cold this winter, you need to evaluate the statement, and the best way is to collect some evidence for the statement. Of course, you need to obtain the evidence before reaching a conclusion. *Note that the example is put into a formal method of reasoning of a premise (what one consider is true) evidence for the premise and a conclusion.*

Premise with evidence
Statement (expect a cold winter) ------- Evidence--------- Conclusion
Expect a cold winter. (premise)
Several meteorologists predict a cold winter. (evidence, like accuracy of predictions)
Therefore, it is likely going to be a cold winter. (conclusion)
Premise with questionable evidence
Expect a cold winter. (premise)
Evidence: My grandmother's hands are hurting her. It happens before we have a cold winter.
Therefore, it's going to be a cold winter. (conclusion?)

Obviously some evidence is better than others. You must ask yourself which information is most reliable and the source of the information. Questions for your students (predictions):
Have your students find evidence on the internet or in books about evidence for the statements below:
Premise: If you don't brush your teeth, they'll fall out
Evidence:
Premise: If you eat too much sugar, you'll look like a big round ball.
Evidence:
Premise: People who sleep eight hours a night are more alert than those who sleep only five hours each night.
Evidence:

Source of information and quality of information may be a life saving experience

Many times you turn to other people to make decisions for you that may affect the quality of your existence and can be a life or death experience. Such people may be your congressional representative or the judges you elect or doctors or educators, to mention a few. There people frequently make decisions for you most of the time without your consent.

Here's what you need to look for in the source of information. Have they published their research or articles in a peer review journal that is accepted by their profession or have they published scholarly papers accepted for publication. Do they belong to professional organization? Do they cite research that is available or other data that can be checked for accuracy?

These people are very important because they may affect your health care, your health insurance, the kind of drugs that are approved for your care. They can approve your hospital or even whether a business is built next to your home. They provide money for your safety, highway control, and money for your children's education. So it's important that they are aware of the data that they use to make informed decisions.

While it may be important to listen to the opinions of others, these people who represent you should also seek out quality and reliable data. If they look at the research of a scholar, they should determine whether others have found the same results that are well qualified. Some of the most reliable data can be found in university libraries, and in the offices of faculty and other researchers, keeping in mind that should not be biased because of contracts with some companies.

If you see a psychologist for marriage counseling, have them provide you with research on the method they will be using. R. B. Stewart once recommended that psychologists have data available when they first meet a client. Same goes for placing children in gifted or special program educations should have data available showing how this affects their children.

Essence

Ke*ep* up your good note taking and teach your children to do the same.

Chapter 17
Learning to Monitor Thinking and Reasoning with Different Scenarios

Now you are going to put things together. You will test yourself and your children on keeping control of their thinking while using reasoning to examine scenarios on problems, persuasion, and arguments. These scenarios should serve as a model for you to generate other scenarios at different grade levels.

Key Words:
Scenario
Mnemonics for monitoring

Q: How do you monitor your thinking to ensure that your biases do not influence your conclusions?
Q: What are some questions you ask yourself when you monitor your thinking?

Practice

You already know that practice makes perfect and neurons that fire together bond together—and they are faster. Practice is more important than you might think, especially if you can keep the mistakes to a minimum. The more variety the practice, the more likely you are to be able to think critically when new and unique situations occur.

Example of a scenario used to monitor thinking
   A scenario is a postulated series of events or a story that may be true of factious with a plot and a series of events. This can be use as practice stories when the learner examines faults or strength of the scenario. The following is an example of using *self-monitoring to evaluate the message from a mother-in-law and how you treat the*

message you receive, including reaching a conclusion and then evaluating the *implications of that conclusion*. Here's the scenario:

Your mother-in-law comes to your house and tells you that if you don't put a stronger rail around your deck, someone is going to get hurt, and if she falls she's going to sue you. That's the message and it's pretty clear. Here's how you should think about this when using the problem-solving steps:

Holy smoke! I really think she means it, and she's the one that's always going out there to do her exercises. She bounces up and down with enough force to shake the plates in the house and make the wine glasses sing. Let me see if I understand everything in her message. It seems that a "stronger" rail is the key element here, and she wants me to make it stronger. (Step 1) Alright, my next step is to collect some information or evidence on the problem. I'll look at the report completed by the structural engineer who inspected the deck last year. She says that the deck is sound and should hold up to 50 people at one time. As for the rail, she said it would hold at least 1,000 pounds of pressure per eight feet (evidence). What are the qualifications of the engineer? She has a master's degree in engineering, belongs to a professional engineering organization, and has an average rating of 4 out of 5 by customers.

What about the qualifications of the mother-in-law? She has no experience with construction, no degree in engineering, belongs to no professional organizations. In other words, she may not know what she is talking about. So the evidence doesn't support what my mother-in-law says. The only other strategy I can think of besides using the data of the experts is to put the rail to a test myself by kicking it and smacking it with my barbell. I'm not going to do that. Also, have I used my *knowledge*? Sure, I remember the engineer's report very well and that my friends leaned against the rail . . . some big, heavy friends (using knowledge).

My conclusion is to ignore my mother-in-law (conclusion). But I must confess, I did not consider my bias, my beliefs (she's a know-it-all), and that I did not try to find out why she thinks the rail is dangerous (open attitude). The long-term effect of my decision to ignore her warning would be that my mother-in-law will hound me every time she sees me until I'm 75 years old and can no longer hear. And what if I'm wrong? I guess I'll be sued . . . so I'm going to have the rail reinforced so a tank couldn't knock it down.

Have your student verbalize or write what might be the unintended consequences of some of their conclusions with other scenarios, and then state what the consequences would be if they are wrong. Then have them say a general statement like, *it pays to look at the unintended consequences of a conclusion and to examine what would happen if my conclusion is wrong.*

Practice problem

Here's a practice reasoning problem for middle and high school youngsters. In this exercise, after reaching a conclusion, your children must consider the long-term implications of their decisions if they are wrong.

Our drinking water is dirty: The *Environmental Working Group* has found that 85% of our drinking water is filled with as many as 300 contaminants. On the other hand, the EPA says that bottled water is not necessarily cleaner than tap water and it is unregulated (unlike tap water) and expensive. Have your students search the internet for answers to this dilemma. If your students do not recognize that water bottles can have an impact on the environment, lead them to consider this. You might want to also look at this web site: http://www.mindbodygreen.com/0-13217/why-you-simply-must-filter-your-water.html

Reasoning to predict the future

When you are trying to figure out exactly what the mother-in-law in the above example is going to do in the future, you certainly need to do some reasoning. One type of reasoning is data-based-reasoning, where you use data to make a prediction just like the open minded individuals did in making predictions about world affairs. The data you could examine might be how many times she has sued other family members or how often she has kept her promise to others. Since most projections about strength of a prediction use probability, you could also consider looking at the degree of variance in the engineer's measurements of strength of the deck.

Monitor thinking to a conclusion

You should want your students to monitor their thinking *with helpful kinds of thoughts*, not just monitor that they are thinking of unrelated events. They should monitor thinking about doing the steps of critical thinking about a specific issue. They should ask themselves questions like those listed in the previous chapters on critical thinking to make certain they are not distorting the information they have recorded in their brains about the problem. *(You may need to review the chapters on critical thinking to make certain your children understand exactly what to monitor.)*

Of course, you should first teach your children the steps already provided for thinking critically, like determining what the message is, what does it want them to do, what evidence is there for the message, and what are the qualifications of the presenter? However, when your children obtain this information, they and they alone are the ones who process the information into their brains. So what they do with the information makes a big difference in determining their conclusions.

Here's an example of the concepts that your children should use to monitor their thinking as they come to conclusions:
Tell your students you are going to give them an example of how a boy named Bali answered the questions below about *the most important things a youngster can do to make good grades in school*:

- Did I jump to a *conclusion* without answering the above questions?
- Did I *massage* the information?
- Did I *embellish* what was remembered? Did I have *tunnel vision*?
- Did I recall the *gist* of the issue?
- Was I *framed?*

Parent/Teacher

Here is your demonstration: Assume that Bali's conclusion to the question of making good grades in school is to *read my assignment, pay attention in class, and do my homework.* Tell your children that the following is an example of how he might have monitored his thinking by asking himself the question about *how thinking can be distorted* as was mentioned in the last two chapters:

- Did I jump to a *conclusion*? I probably did, because that's what everybody says, so it must be true . . . wait a minute, maybe there's something else . . . like trying to understand every sentence I read and . . . several other things.
- Did I *massage* the information? No information or evidence was given. It was just a question. (This is checking your biases.)
- Did I *embellish* the information? Of course not! What about *tunnel vision*? I don't think so. Now that I think about it, I may have just ignored other information because it is different than what most teachers say.
- Have I recalled the *gist*—what is generally thought about making good grades or is there some more specific evidence for making good grades? Maybe there is. You don't just pay attention; you should do some other things. I remember that making learning meaningful is important and by summarizing and organizing, I can learn more.
- Did the questions *frame* me to answer in this way? It was presented by a teacher. I wonder how I would answer it if Bill, my buddy, had asked me?

If students are going use the concepts listed above, they must know what they mean and how to remember them. What follows is a method to teach them to monitor their thinking to ensure that they do not distort the information:

Parent/Teacher

Now it is time to make certain your children know the concepts mentioned above. Ask them to remember the concepts for monitoring their thinking and give examples. Repeat this until the students remember the concepts. You may need to use mnemonics to

208

help them remember the first letter of each concept, like c (conclusion), me (massage and embellish) g (gist), f (frame). This makes the mnemonic of "see(c) me (m-e) gist or get (g) framed (f). "*See me gist (or) get framed.*" Make a better example of a mnemonic or even better have them make a mnemonic, if you can. *(Make certain you have taught them how to use mnemonics as described in the chapter on learning facts.)*

Teachers
Students recall the concepts and give examples
You may need to have your children write the mnemonics for the concepts (c m e g f) on a slip of paper placed on their desks or laptops (or wherever they can see them) to help them remember the concepts that will help them to make accurate conclusions.

You tell your students, "This time you tell me how to answer the questions (c m e g f) about your thinking after listening to the following debate and before making a conclusion:"

• *Brooklyn* tells you to keep away from German shepherd dogs. Their bite is so strong that it is equal to smashing your hand with a heavy hammer. They are very dangerous. They are used as guard dogs, and the police use them to capture criminals. They are ranked as one of the 10 most dangerous dogs, according to several sites on the internet. Remember Sherry; she was bitten by a German Shepherd, and it broke the bones in three of her fingers. You will recall she was in the hospital for several days and had that big bandage on her hand for a long time. She had several operations. Stay away from those dogs!

• *Mr. Wu* tells you he is a trainer of dogs. He said German Shepherds aren't any more dangerous than other large dogs, but their bite is powerful. German Shepherds rank behind Chows, Pit bulls, Doberman Pinchers, Rhodesian Ridgebacks, Siberian Huskies, and Rottweilers as the top 10 most dangerous dogs. However, the American breed is less aggressive than some foreign breeds. It is important to understand that how dogs are treated in early life determines their temperament to a large degree. Socialize with your dogs to make them friendly and let them experience other dogs when young and you'll likely have friendly German shepherds.

<u>Children</u>
Have your student answer the "c me get framed" questions. Here's how your students might answer the questions:

- Did I jump to a *conclusion* without answering the "c me get framed" questions? No, I thought about what both said and considered what might influence my decision.
- Did I *massage* any of the information? Maybe, because of what happened to Sherry was unpleasant.
- Did I *embellish* their danger from what was remembered (my inferences) about them? No, Mr. Wu explained why some dogs are dangerous and some are not. What about tunnel vision? I'll read what they said again . . . just in case I missed something.
- Did I recall the *gist* of what is known about German Shepherds? Sure, everyone has a general idea of what German shepherds are like.
- Was I *framed* in answering the questions above? Yes, I was a little because I knew Sherry and remember she hurt so much.

Arguments

If you watch news on television, you'll see all kinds of arguments. You might even have an argument with your friends, relatives, and even your spouse. And if you look on the internet, you'll see a great deal of examples of analyzing arguments. It's not unusual for tests that measure critical thinking to use questions about arguments.

It should come as no surprise that you analyze arguments in the same way you analyze the messages you receive. Here's an example of an argument that could be analyzed by elementary school children.

Your students could use the questions that follow the arguments below to determine whether they monitored their thinking as they do some critical thinking.

Mother said, "You must eat your vegetables because they are healthy. You will get used to the taste after you eat them awhile. They help build strong bodies and keep your brains functioning. Your skin will look healthier and you won't be fat."

Father said, "You need to eat more red meat. It's filled with proteins and minerals that you need for growth of muscles and bones. You'll grow strong and straight. Vegetables are for sissies. Look how smooth my face looks and look how big I am compared to your mother."

Mother replied, "A healthy diet of vegetables, fruit, as a small portion of meat have been found to prevent heart disease and colon cancer,", according to the United States Food and Drug Administration, If you want to live a healthy life, you better eat more of these healthy foods. You won't get so fat then. Just look at your dad with that big belly! His heart must beat harder to supply blood and nutrients to the fat part of his body and that's likely to 'do him in."

Father replied, "I'm the picture of health. I haven't been to the doctor in years and I'm already 30 years of age. I say just taste some rich-red meat with a little bit of fat between the lean and then taste some broccoli. Your taste tells you what is good for you; but I must admit that candy tastes good and it's not good for you. I read in the *Knoxville New Sentinel* where babies can smell bad foods and turn away. That's why I don't eat cooked cabbage!"

   Ask your children to do the following:
- Define any words you do not know (use the dictionary or web).
- Make certain you monitor your thinking as you answer these questions using an open attitude.
- Make certain you discover what the debaters are contending (exactly what do they mean?).
- Make certain you examine the qualifications of each person.
- Make certain you find the evidence for their positions.
- Make certain you place the information into a premise, evidence (inference), and conclusion.
   Did you collect evidence and see the likely conclusion?
- Make a conclusion, consider long term implications, and explain why.

Start Small

Of course you are not going to be able to teach your preschool and elementary school youngsters all these skills to critical thinking at one time, but you can teach them by reducing these skills into parts. For example, you can get your preschool youngsters to simply compare things: like which food is healthier? An orange or a candy bar? You can list the advantages and disadvantages and then have them make a decision as to which one is healthier using such steps as "what might be the long-term consequences?" By the 5*th* grade they *should be able to use their laptops to look up the evidence, and by middle school they could question the evidence and whether they are influenced by their biases.*

For more practice in critical thinking, go to http.//skillstocriticalthinking.com

Keep in mind:
By the yard it is very hard,
But by the inch it's a cinch. (Author unknown.)

Essence

Be certain to make organized notes on this chapter while trying to capture the essence, and don't forget to answer the questions at the beginning. They are important.

Chapter 1 Paremts and Teachers Together

Page 1	Statement	Reference (Notes)

1 And before they are off to school: (n. n.). (2014*). Bright horizons.* How to develop critical thinking skills in kids. Retrieved from https://www.brighthorizons.com/family-resources/e-family-news/2014-developing-critical-thinking-skills-in-children/

1 Parents can and do teach critical thinking: (June 6, 2011). From Price-Mitchell, M. *Roots of Action*, How to grow your child's mind. Retrieved from http://www.rootsofaction.com/critical-thinking-ways-to-improve-your-childs-mind-this-summer/

Bartels, D. (2013). CT is best taught outside the classroom, CT is a teachable sill best taught outside the classroom. Retrieved from https://www.scientificamerican.com/article/critical-thinking-best-taught-outside-classroom/CT

Hayes, D. (August 8, 2014). Let's stop trying to teach students critical thinking. The Conversation. Retrieved from http://theconversation.com/lets-stop-trying-to-teach-students-critical-thinking-30321

1   Stacy Schiff, in her book the *Witches*: Schiff, S. (2015). *The Witches.* Back Bay Books/ Little Brown and Company, Hatcher Book Group, 9.

1 They will need to evaluate their own thinking: Paul, R. W., & Elder, L. (2002). *Critical Thinking: Tools for Taking Charge of Your Professional and Personal Life,* Person Education, Inc. Upper Saddle River, NJ

2 Why are four-year olds: Christian, B. and Griffiths, T. (2016). *Algorithms to Live B.* Henry Holt and Company. 103

3 Words related to learning: Springer, Marilee, (June 2013). ASCD Teaching the Critical Vocabulary of the Common Core. Retrieved from http://www.ascd.org/publications/books/113040/chapters/What-Does-the-Research-Say-About-Vocabulary¢.aspx Also, cited in *A diversified Portfolio Model of Adaptability*, Siddharth, C. & Leong, Frederick T. L. (2016). Michigan State University. *American Psychologist*. 71. 847-862.

4 When babies are born their . . . . and when brains are pruned: Huttenlocher, P. (August 26,2013). Retrieved from *https://books.google.com/books/about/Neural_Plasticity.html?id=HXmRlT fSdYQC&hl=en*

4 Suzanne Bouffard in her book, *Most Important Year s,* says that children's brains develop at a much faster: Begley, S. (September 4, 2017). *TIME Magazine*, The advantage of universal per-K. 24

4 There's no reasoning without words: Paul, R. W. (2002). Thinking is to create meaning. *Critical Thinking: Tools for Taking Charge of Your Professional and Personal Life.* Person Education, Inc. Upper Saddle River, N.J. 40

4 Concepts form the basis for every skill: Paul, R. W. (2002). Thinking is to create meaning. *Critical Thinking: Tools for Taking Charge of Your Professional and Personal Life.* Person Education, Inc. Upper Saddle River, N.J. 78-81.

5 This term "using your head" is often called a megacognitive skill: (n .n.). (n. d). Studypool. (Metacognition is the ability to use ones' prior knowledge to plan a strategy.) Retrieved from https://www.studypool.com/discuss/2810867/Metacognition-is-one-s-ability-to-use-prior-knowledge-to-plan-a-strategy-Psychology-Discussion-help

5   Even practicing debating can improve critical thinking Dewar, Gwen (2009-2012) Retrieved from www.parentingscience.com/teachingcriticalthinking.html Teaching critical thinking.

7 A stimulating environment can alter your youngster's brains: (n/n). (September 2013). *Monitor on Psychology* .(It has been found that children who practice string instruments have added brain growth.)

*Bryck, Richard L. & Fisher, Phillip A., (Feb March 2012). *American Psychologist.* 68, 87-100. (Training the brain.)

Nisbett, R. E., Aronson, J., Blair, C., Dickens, F., William; Flynn, J., Halpern, D. F., & Turkheimer, E. (February/March, 2012). New Findings and theoretical developments, *American Psychologists*, 67. 136. (Environment influence on intelligence.)

Drubach, D. (2000). *The Brain Explained.* Upper Saddle River, NJ: Prentice-Hall, Inc. (There appears to be at least two types of modifications that occur in the brain with learning: A change in the internal structure of the neurons, the most notable being in the area of synapses, and an increase in the number of synapses between neurons.)

Le Storti, A. J. (2002). ERIC Critical thinking at home and at school. How might parents and teachers become better teachers of critical thinking? Retrieved from https://eric.ed.gov/?id=EJ653802 Understanding our gifted.14. 6-9. (The need to model critical thinking is stressed.)

7 There is a section of your children's brains called that respond to events they consider to be positive, and they will be motivated to seek the stimulation of these areas of the brain, be it chocolate or success in learning: (n. n). (June 2017). Memory Skill. *Monitor on Psychology.* In Brief, 10. (From a study in *Neuron.)*

9 Now intelligent machines have used the same method of stimulating your brains to get you and your children "hooked" on using their machines. Edwards, H. S. (April 23, 2018). The masters of mind control. *TIME Magazine* 191, 30-37.

9 Make certain your notes are precise and concise. Bui, D. & McDaniel, M. (June 2015) *Educational Research Report on Cognition.* 4. 129-135. (Students who received outlines and diagrams had enhanced learning and also had fewer and better quality notes.)

Chapter 2 Learning Basic Comprehension

12 Your teacher should have told you time and time again, Swanson, L. H. & Deshler, D. (March/April 2003). *Journal of Learning Disabilities*, 36. 124–135. (Instructing Adolescents with Learning Disabilities: Converting a Meta-Analysis to Practice. Advanced organizers build a scaffold in which to hang information)

12 Comprehend means to: (n .n). (n. d). Understand the meaning. Retrieved from http://www.dictionary.com/browse/comprehending (Comprehend is to understand the nature of or meaning of.)

14 A strong relationship between vocabulary and comprehension: Hart, B & Risley, T. (1995*). Meaningful differences*. Baltimore, MD. Brookes.

Nisbett, R..E., Aronson, J. B., Clancy. D., William; Flynn, J.; Halpern, DF., & Turkheimer, E. (February &March 2012).*American Psychologists*, 67. 136. (Children of professional parents have higher vocabularies than working class.)

15 Children of upper-class families: Pinker, S. (2015). *NY Times*. Can Student Have Too Much Tech? Retrieved from https://iblog.dearbornschools.org/hosambasha/wp-content/uploads/sites/2274/2016/10/ Tech-article-4.pdf (Babies born to low-income parents spend at least 40 percent of their waking hours in front of a screen — more than twice the time spent by middle-class babies.).

Chiese, S., & Voes. (July 10, 2015). *Reading Resources.* This Reading Mama. Reading Comprehension Resources. Retrieved from https://thisreadingmama.com/reading-comprehension-resources/ (Positive correlation between vocabulary and reading comprehension.)

15 Vincent Sheean about Winston Churchill: Sheean V. (June 1958). Churchill. *American Heritage.*

16 Questions within a lesson: Anderson, R.C. & Faust, G. W. (1973). *Educational Psychology: The Science of Instruction and Learning*. New York: Dodd Mead and Co. 128.
 (Questions interspaced in a lesson twice as effective in learning as questions at the end.)

Bangert-Drowns, R. L., Kulik, R., & Chen-Lin C. (08/09/2013). Effects of Frequent Classroom Testing. *The Journal of Educational Research*, 85. 89-99

Dempster, F. N. (1992). Using Tests to Promote Learning: A neglected Classroom Resource *Journal of Research and Development.*

17 Later, you will be shown research that shows how moving your lips when answering increases learning: (n. n.). (December 2015). *Monitory on Psychology*. Repeating something aloud to another person may boost memory.46, 19.   (University of Montreal. *Consciousness and Cognition*, November.)

17 Must retrieve the components and then put them together to recall the memory. Di Solvo, D. (2011). *What makes your brain happy and why you should do the opposite*, Prometheus Books. (Definition of schema "a mental map of concepts that hangs together by association" 50; guides our attention to evaluate new information. 51)

19 **Show and Tell Your Students the Question and Answer:** (n. n.). (n. d.). Tripod. An Outline of Direct Instruction, Lesson Design. Retrieved from http://members.tripod.com/teaching_is_reaching/lesson_design.htmhttp:// members.tripod.com/teaching_is_reaching/lesson_design.htm, 19 (Explicit)

19 Direct instruction: (basic steps) (n/n). (n/d). Tripod. An Outline of Direct Instruction, Lesson Design. Retrieved from http://members.tripod.com/teaching_is_reaching/lesson_design.htm

Adams, G., & Engelmann, S. (1996). *Research on Direct Instruction*: In-depth and Beyond. *Educational Achievement Systems*, Seattle (Research on Direct Instruction compared to other programs.)

Goeke, J. L., (2009) *Explicit Instruction: A Framework for Meaningful Direct Teaching*, Merrill, Upper Saddle River, New JerseyColumbus, Ohio

(n. n.). (2015). Project Follow Through *National Institute of Direct Instruction*. Retrieved from http://www.nifdi.org/research/ (The most extensive educational experiment ever conducted. Beginning in 1968 under the sponsorship of the federal government, it was charged with determining the best way of teaching at-risk children from kindergarten throgh grade 3. Over 200,000 children in 178 communities were included in the study, and 22 different models of instruction were compared.)

(n .n.). (n. d).Tripod. An Outline of Direct Instruction, Lesson Design. Retrieved from http://members.tripod.com/teaching_is_reaching/lesson_design.htm

Millet, J. R. (July 2011). Retrieved from https://repository.asu.edu/attachments/57034/content/Millett_asu_0010E_1 0994.pdf (Reading vocabulary was found to be a strong predictor of reading comprehension.)

18 Memories are stored in your brain in a variety of places: Wesson, K. (Fall 2001). What the brain Research Tells Us About Learning, www.nais.org/publications/ismagizinearticle.cfm?) 1-12 (each part of what is learned is transmitted to different parts of the brain and the reconnect.)

Schscter, D. (November 2012). *American Psychologist, 10,* 603-4 (Memory is stored on neurons in your brain and they are connected into schema with other neurons.)

18 Schemata is like a mental map that hangs together by association.

19 Feedback is nothing more than providing information on the correctness of a response: (n. n.). (Oct 2013). *Monitor on Psychology,* 44, (9), 15-16 (feedback have high expectations and "I know you can reach them.")

Salas, S. B. & Dickinson, D. J. (1990). The effects of feedback and three different types of corrections on student learning, *Journal of Human Behavior and Learning,* 7, 13-20.

19 The more immediate the feedback, the more effective is the feedback: DiSalvo, D. (2011). *What makes your brain happy and why you should do the opposite.* Prometheus Books. 108 &186-7. (Improve learning if feedback is prompt. The amount of neural activity, the stronger the connection will continue to be.)

Hake, R. (1998). Retrieved from https://en.wikipedia.org/wiki/Active_learning **"(--doing something besides being passive—"Richard Hake. reviewed data from over 6,000)**

23 Criterion reasoning is: (n. n.). (n. d.) *Changing Minds*. Types of Reasoning. Retrieved from http://changingminds.org/disciplines/argument/types_reasoning/types_reasoning.htm (comparing against)

24 You can also find more information on this activity and even a letter to parents about participating at: Fermilab, S. D., & Franzen, P. (n.d.). Science Lines. *The Science Journal:* Writing and inquiry development. Retrieved from http://ed.fnal.gov/trc_new/sciencelines_online/fall97/activity_inserts.html (how to keep a science journal and letter to parents about the journal.)

Chapter 3 Learning Deeper Comprehension

28 Deeper comprehension: Myer, R. E. (November 2008). *American Psychologist*, 63, 761-769. "Deep learning depends on the learner's cognitive processing during learning, e.g. selecting, organizing and integrating." (The learner selects a channel visual, sound, pictorial to receive the information.)

29 An inference is a first step: (n. n). (n. d.) Retrieved from https://www.bing.com/search?q=what+is+an+inference&form=EDGHPT&qs=DA&cvid=20f514811a794b4087381d0c08b2d93f&cc=US&setlang=en-US (An inference is based on evidence and reasoning.)

Kispal, A. (2008). Effective Teaching of Inference Skill in Reading. *Literature Review, Research Report* DCSF-RR031. Retrieved from http://files.eric.ed.gov/fulltext/ED501868.pdf

30 This is one of Aesop's fables: Bennett, W. J. (1993). The Dog and His Shadow. *The Book of Virtues.* Simon & Schuster

**31 *Maugham, William Summerset:* *(n. n.).(January 1, 1933). Death Speaks. Genius.* Retrieved from https://genius.com/William-somerset-maugham-death-speaks-annotated

33 Summarizing is: Annis, L. F. (1985). Student-generated paragraph summaries and the informational processing theory of prose learning. *Journal of Experimental Education*, 5. ("Summarizing is a condensation of information, capturing the gist of a paragraph or several --- to facilitate the learning of prose.. Learning is facilitated because a person version of this text is more likely to be related to "—what one already knows.)

34 Why does summarizing help with comprehension? (n .n.). (n. d.). CIERA Research based principles. Summarizing recommended for comprehension. Improving the Reading of America's Children: 10 Research-Based Principles. http://www.ciera.org/library/instresrc/principles/

Annis, F. L. (1985). Student generated paragraph summaries and the information-process theory of prose learning. *Journal of Experimental Education*. 54, 4-10

Annis, L. F. (1985). Student-generated paragraph summaries and the informational processing theory of prose learning. *Journal of Experimental Education*. 54.

34 Elizabeth Long did a study to: Long, E. W. (1985). The effects of metacomprehension on college student achievement. Unpublished doctoral dissertation. The University of Tennessee, Knoxville.

35 Organizing is noting the relations between concepts or ideas: Dickinson, D. J. & O'Connell, D. (March/April 1990). Effects of Quality and Quantity of Study on Students Grades, *Journal of Educational Research*. 83. (Organizing more effective than total study time.)

35 Doris Goodman describes Lincoln's: Goodwin, D. K., (2005) *Teams of Rivals*. Simon & Schuster. 51-53.

38 According to *Scientific American*, your brain has about one billion neurons: Reber, P. (May 2010). *Scientific America.* What is the memory capacity of the Human brain? Retrieved from https://www.scientificamerican.com/article/what-is-the-memory-capacity/

38 How do you know that your brain has created a memory map? Holley, C. D., Dansereau, D. F., McDonald, B. A., Garland, J. C., & Collins, K. W. (1979). Evaluation of a hierarchical mapping technique as an aid to prose processing. *Contemporary Educational Psychology, 4.* 227-237. (Organizing, networking-- is a listing of major concepts and their relationship to each other.)

38 In 2016 the *New York Tribune* published an article stating that 97 new locations of mappings of the brain have been found, bringing the total to 180: Zimmer, C. (2016). Undated brain map identify nearly 100 new regions. Retrieved from https://www.nytimes.com/2016/07/21/science/human-connectome-brain-map.html

39 *Providing outlines and diagrams will also increase student learning:* Bui, D. & McDaniel, M. (June 2015) *Educational Research Report on Cognition.* 4. 129-135. (Providing students with diagrams improved learning.)

Chapter 4 Learning Concrete Concepts

43 Experts say that concepts are "like the air we breathe" they are "everywhere," and are "essential to our life: Paul, R. W. & Elder, L. (2002). *Critical Thinking: Tools for Taking Charge of Your Professional and Personal Life.* Person Education, Inc. Upper Saddle River. NJ. 78-81.

44 Webster defines a concept as "-- an idea or thought, esp. a *generalized idea of a thing or class of things; abstract notion:*" (n .n.). (n. d.). https://www.merriam-webster.com/dictionary/concept

Genter, D. (2016). Language as a Cognitive Tool Kit: How Language Supports Rational Thought. *American Psychologist.* 71, 650-657.

Paul, R. W. & Elder, L. (2002) *Critical Thinking: Tools for Taking Charge of Your Professional and Personal Life.* Person Education, Inc. Upper Saddle River, NJ.

44 There are three major kinds of concepts: Hastings, K.W., & Xu Xu. (2005). *Cognitive Science* 29. 719-736 Content Difference for Concrete and Abstract Concepts. Retrieved from http://csjarchive.cogsci.rpi.edu/2005v29/5/s15516709HCOG0000_33/s155 16709HCOG0000_33.pdf

44 Concrete concepts can be seen and are usually nouns. We'll call these "visible or concrete concepts: (n. n.). (2018). DB Difference Between. Difference between abstract and concrete in language. Retrieved from http://www.differencebetween.info/difference-between-abstract-and-concrete-in-language (Concrete nouns can usually be experienced by the five senses.)

46 Concepts have key feathers —concepts have critical features:
Lefrancois, G. (1972). *Psychological Theories and Human Leaning.*
Books/Cole Publishing company, Monterey, California. 163 (critical features --distinguishable variation from event to event --- representation of related things is a concept. Those attributes that define an object are called *critical.*)

Concepts. Lefrancois, G. (1972). *Psychological Theories and Human Leaning.* Books/Cole Publishing company, Monterey, California 163 (critical features --distinguishable variation from event to event." "--representation of related things is a concept. Those attributes that define an object are called *critical.*)

52 A set means a predisposition to look for certain things and it can be taught by practice. 32-3 Being Set: Kindra, C. (n. d.). Very Well. Retrieved from https://www.verywell.com/what-is-a-perceptual-set-2795464 (Very Well, What is a Perceptual Set? Predisposed to perceive things in a certain way. ---tend to notice only certain aspects ---- and ignore others---. Can be influenced by interest and motives.)

Chapter 5 Learning Abstract Concepts

56 Abstract concepts are just in your mind: (n. n.). (n. d.) Definition of comprehending. Retrieved from http://www.dictionary.com/browse/comprehending (Comprehend is to understand the nature of or meaning of.)

Burner, J. S., Goodnow, J.J., & Austin, G.A. (1956). *A study of thinking*, New York: Wiley ". 1. (categorize is to --- group objects or events and people around us into classes.)

56 *Justice" is defined as a just action or treatment:* (n. n.) (n. d.) Justice. Retrieved from https://www.bing.com/search?q=defination%20of%20justice&qs=n&form =QBRE&sp=-1&pq=defination%20of%20justice&sc=8-21&sk=&cvid=9A816A95B7F7462CAFE69A82CA4FE93C

58 Let's start with a definition of positive reinforcement: (n. n.) (n. d.) Positive reinforcement. Retrieved from http://www.dictionary.com/browse/positive-reinforcement

61 Discriminative method: Salas, S. B. & Dickinson, D. J. (1990). The effects of feedback and three different types of corrections on student learning, *Journal of Human Behavior and Learning,* 7, 13-20.

60 Process concepts are also abstract concepts with some steps or rules: Medin, D. L., Lynch, E. B., & Karen O. (2000). Solomon Department of Psychology, Northwestern University, Evanston, Illinois 60208; e-mail:medin@nwu.edu, elynch@nwu.edu, Retrieved from k-solomon@nwu.edu Annual. Review of Psychology (2000) 51:121–1470084–6570/00/0201–0121$12.00 **121** (ARE THERE KINDS OF CONCEPTS?)

60 *Using a great number of examples: (n. n). (August 2014.) Instructional strategies for Educators.* Retrieved from http://www.ecu.edu/cs-educ/TQP/upload/ISLES-S-Concept-Procedural-Aug2014.pdf

63 Cherish means to "protect and care for someone lovingly: (n. n.). (n. d). *Free Dictionary.* Retrieved from https://www.bing.com/search?q=free+dictionary+chearish&form=EDGSPH&mkt=en-us&httpsmsn=1&refig=32dab44ff86d4cb68151e2965d965827&sp=-1&ghc=1&pq=free+dictionary+chearish&sc=0-24&qs=n&sk=&cvid=32dab44ff86d4cb68151e2965d965827

63 Blog Life: Kingsley, I. (n. d.). examples of cherish. Retrieved from http://theboldlife.com/2008/10/how-to-cherish-people-and-relationships/

64 Two types of reasoning here: (n. .n.). (n. d.). What is analytical reasoning. Retrieved from https://www.reference.com/business-finance/analytical-research-94534a536bf46028?qo=contentSimilarQuestions

Chapter 6 Learning Facts

66 Your students might chunk (or reduce) the information: Pinola, M. (Sept 26 2012). *Life hackers.* Improve your memory with the chunking technique. Retrieved from https://lifehacker.com/5946606/improve-your-memory-with-the-chunking-technique.

66 Facts are indisputable: Free Dictionary. (2003-2018). Indisputable facts. Retrieved from http://encyclopedia2.thefreedictionary.com/Indisputable+Facts

68 How your brain works: Anderson, J. R. (2000). New York: John Wiley & Sons. Learning and Memory Short-Term Memory. Retrieved from *Learning and memory: An integrated approach*

(n. n.). (2010). Big Dog & Little Dog's Performance juxtaposition. Learning and Memory. Retrieved from http://www.nwlink.com/~donclark/hrd/learning/memory.html (In cognitive psychology, there is one memory system, but it is normally divided into three functions for storage: sensory, short-term (often called *working*, and long-.)

Kindra, C.. (September 2017). Verywell. What is short memory and how long does it last? Retrieved from http://psychology.about.com/od/memory/f/short-term-memory.htm (short term memory lasts 20-30 seconds).

Digitale, E. (August 2014). Stanford Medicine. New light sheds light on how children's brains memorize facts. Retrieved from.https://med.stanford.edu/news/all-news/2014/08/new-research-sheds-light-on-how-childrens-brains-memorize-facts.html (New brain-imaging research gives the first evidence drawn from a longitudinal study to explain how the brain reorganizes itself as children learn math facts. The results, published online Aug. 17 in Nature Neuroscience,)

70   Children who sleep more make better grades: Locker, M. (January 13, 2015). Time. Let your kids sleep more for better grades. Retrieved from http://time.com/3663796/for-better-grades-let-your-kids-sleep-more/

70 Your students might chunk (or reduce) the information: Pinola, M. (Sept 26, 2012). *Life hackers*. Improve your memory with the chunking technique. Retrieved from https://lifehacker.com/5946606/improve-your-memory-with-the-chunking-technique.

Kolb, D. (n. d.). Information Instruction: Strategies for Library and Information Professionals. Retrieved from http://eduscapes.com/instruction/6.htm (Organize material into reasonable chucks.)

71 A mnemonic is anything that can be used as an aid for memorizing information:
Congos, D. (2006). University of Central Florida. Types of Mnemonics for Better Memory
Retrieved from
http://www.learningassistance.com/2006/january/mnemonics.html

72 adjusting the curriculum: 47-8 Dickinson, D. J. & Butt, J. A. (Oct. 1989). The effects of success and failure on the on-task behavior of high and low achieving students. *Education and Treatment of Children*. (When students who were off-task were given math problems that they could do, they suddenly stayed on-task.)

73 Self-efficacy is the belief that you or your children have the confidence to successfully learn new: Bandura, A. (1977). *Self-efficacy: The exercise of control*. New York: NY Freeman. Also cited in A diversified Portfolio Model of Adaptability. Chandrea, S. & Leong. F. T. L. (2016). Michigan State University. *America Psychologist*, 71, 847-862.

73 **It can change the chemical composition of your bloodstream as well as altering the chemistry of your brain:**
Popova, M. **(2012). Why success breeds success: The science of the winner effect.** Retrieved from http://www.brainpickings.org/index.php/2012/08/09/jonh-coates-hour-between-dog-and-wolf-winner-effect/69 (Quoting John Coates: "Tennis players who win the first match have a 60% chance of winning the second match.")

73 When male athletes win an event, their testosterone spikes. This gives them a:
Popova, M. (2012). **Why success breeds success: The science of the winner effect.** Retrieved from http://www.brainpickings.org/index.php/2012/08/09/jonh-coates-hour-between-dog-and-wolf-winner-effect/ 69

74 Charles Duhigg in his book *The Power of Habit* states, "A huge body of research has shown that small wins have enormous power, an influence disproportionate to the accomplishments of the victories themselves." Duhigg, C. (2012). *The Power of Habit*. Random House, New York.

74 Social consequences can be smiles, praise, and just talking to someone: Riggio, R. E. (Jun 2012). There's magic in your smile. How smiling affects your brain. Retrieved from https://www.psychologytoday.com/us/blog/cutting-edge-leadership/201206/there-s-magic-in-your-smile

74 Review past learning: (n. n.). (n. d). Reviewing what, why, and how. Retrieved from http://www.reviewing.co.uk/_review.htm (n .n.). (n. d.). Mind strategies. Review strategies. Retrieved from http://www.reviewing.co.uk/_review.htm

74 **Review is a form of practice***:* Winnerman, L. (October 2016). Brain development. *Monitor in Psychology*. Brief.47, 9. Retrieved from http://lifehacker.com/the-science-of-practice-what-happens-when-you-learn-a-510255025 published in *the Journal of Neuroscience.* (What practice is actually doing is helping the brain optimize for this set of coordinated activities, through a process called myelination**.**)

74 Neurons that fire together, wire together: DiSalvo, D. (2011). *What makes your brain happy and why you should do the opposite.* Prometgeus books, 108,186-7. (Improve learning if feedback is prompt. The amount of neural activity, the stronger the connection will continue to be.) (What practice is actually doing is helping the brain optimize for this set of coordinated activities, through a process called myelination**.**)

Sterling C., **A.** (Aug 28, 2014). *Demand Media. Globalpost.* Homework's effects on grades in high school. (Homework can raise high school grades, because work outside of class promotes learning and develops skills. (The Center for Public Education reviewed two decades of research on the benefits of homework, finding that high school students can improve their grades by doing 1 1/2 to two hours of homework a night. More than two hours of homework a night could be too much, however, and the benefit of homework for younger students is still not clearly proven.)

75 Researchers Larry Coleman and Aige Guo, Aige & Coleman, Larry of the University of Toledo in 2014 found that practice played a significant role with children highly passionate to learn: Coleman, Laurence J. & Guo, A. (June 2013). Exploring children's passion for learning in six domains, *Journal of Education for the Gifted*. Retrieved from http://journals.sagepub.com/doi/abs/10.1177/0162353213480432

75 *they should do it again with homework*: Sterling, C. A. (Aug 28, 2014). *Demand Media. Globalpost.* Homework's effects on grades in high school. 48. *Journal of Research and in Personality* and later in 2018 published in the Briefs of *Monitor in Psychology* found that doing homework: (Homework can raise high school grades, because work outside of class promotes learning and develops skills. The Center for Public Education reviewed two decades of research on the benefits of homework, finding that high school students can improve their grades by doing 1 1/2 to two hours of homework a night. More than two hours of homework a night could be too much, however, and the benefit of homework for younger students is still not clearly proven.)

75 Brian Christian and Tom Griffiths in their book *Algorithms to Live By*, **who describe a juggler:** Christian, B. & Griffiths, T. (2016). *Algorithms to Live By*, Henry Holt and Company**.**

Logan, G. D. (2017). Taking control of cognition: an instance perspective on acts of control. American Psychologist. 72 (9), 875-884. (Multitasking is often operationalized in task switching experiments, 879.)

76 According Yuval Noah Harari author of *Saipan: A Brief History of Humankind:* Noah Harari, Y. (2016). *Homo Saipan. A brief history of humankind.* Vintage. *122.*

Chapter 7 Learning to Think about Learning

80 Beliefs are more or less permanent thoughts that are held dearly, strongly, and perpetually: Kotsos, T. (January 2009). *Dream manifesto.* Retrieved from http://www.dreammanifesto.com/habits-life-answer-permanent-change.html (Your habits are the products of your beliefs.)

81   Metacognitive strategies: (n. n.). (September 3, 2015). Inclusive School Network. Metacognitive Strategies. Retrieved from http://inclusiveschools.org/metacognitive-strategies/
(A process to help students think about their thinking---understand the way they learn.)

81 Thinking is that verbal dialogue that goes on in your mind all the time: Paul, R. W. & Elder, L. (2002). *Critical Thinking: Tools for Taking Charge of Your Professional and Personal Life.* Person Education, Inc. Upper Saddle River, NJ. 40. (Thinking is to create meaning.)

Graesser, A. C. (November 2011). Learning, Thinking, and Emoting with Discourse Technologies. *American Psychologist.* 66. 46-757.

Louis, D. Madison-Harris R. Muoneke, A. & Times, C. (January 2015). *American Institute for Research.* Using data to guide instruction. Retrieved from
 http://www.sedl.org/pubs/sedl-letter/v22n02/using-data.html

82 Self talk can make a difference: Breadsley, C. (2013). Toggle Navigation. Does motivational self talk improve performance? 1-6.

82 All children need objective feedback: Mellers, B. (January 2016). Using data in problem solving. Esther derby associates. Retrieved from http://www.estherderby.com/2016/01/using-data-in-problem-solving.html

82   Data is some kind of *records* like grades: (n. n.). (January 2018). Merriam Webster. Data.
Retrieved from https://www.merriam-webster.com/dictionary/data **(**Factual information, such as measurement or statistics)

83 And as a consequence, many become somewhat narcissistic—that is, they think they are privileged: Goleman, D. (October, 1995). *Emotional Intelligence.* Bantam Book, 20. (Recent research cast doubt of this study. See *Monitor on Psychology* (n. n.). (Feb 2018). 16. Citing a study in *Psychology Science* it was found when misunderstood items were adjusted the new study indicated that college students' narcissism has not increased.

83 Become materialists' seekers: (n .n.). (March 2015). *Monitor in Psychology.* Parent who use material goods to reward or punish their children may be setting those children up got difficulty in adulthood. 22-3 (citing work by the University of Missouri and Illinois at Chicago.)

83 You did it: Education world. Dirksen, A. (2012). Education World. 99 ways to say 'Very Good." Retrieved from

http://www.educationworld.com/a_curr/curr375.shtml ('you did it,"
"now you have it." "Aren't you proud of yourself?" "Now you've figured
it out.")

86 Rules and Beliefs Cause Your Students to Behave: Mahoney, M.
(1974).*Cognition and Behavior Modification*. Ballinger Publishing
Company, Cambridge, Mass.

Mahoney, M. (1974).*Cognition and Behavior Modification*
Ballinger Publishing Company. Cambridge, Mass. Belief, Counter-
Control, and Choice. 227-252 (--belief is a rule of action—" 229.
Mahoney. 237. Beliefs – very resistant to extinction.)

**90 As soon as your children can write have them write in a
notebook:** Travers, C. (September 2017). *Monitor on Psychology*, 57.(
Also having to write how you are doing based on data will help you to be
objective about your progress and make you feel responsible.)

**91 A study published in the journal of *Science* in 2009 found when
students were asked to write   the usefulness and value of what was
being taught before taking a 10th grade science class:** Akcaogula, M.,
Rosenberg, J. M., Rannellucci, J. & Schwartz, C. V. (2017*). Journal of
Educational Research*. Retrieved from
https://www.sciencedirect.com/science/article/pii/S0883035517308492

**91   Here's how to commence to teach reasons (rules) and general
reasons (beliefs):** Mahoney, M. (1974). *Cognition and Behavior
Modification* Ballinger Publishing Company, Cambridge, Mass.   (Citing
Meichenbaum (1969) self-instruction.)

Mahoney, M.. (1974). *Cognition and Behavior Modification*
Ballinger Publishing Company, Cambridge. (Individuals often exhibit less
autonomic distress when they perceive themselves as having some
potential control over unpleasant experiences.) 215.

**93 Participants' brains that practiced positive thinking in as little as
two months:** McKenna, P. (2010). *I Can Make You Confident*. Sterling.
90.(Brain change in two months)

**94 *Behavior Modification* found that elementary school children who
had use token reinforces when:** Dickinson, D. J. (1974). But what
happens when you take that reinforcement away? *Psychology in the*

Schools. 11, 158-160. (Reprinted in *Great Experiments in Behavior Modification* by J. W. Willis and D. Giles, Hacket Publishing Company.)

94 Study described in David Goleman's book *Emotional Intelligence*, students were brought into a room one at a time and found another student waiting who was an actor unknown to them: Goleman, D. (October, 1995). *Emotional Intelligence.* Bantam Book.

94 Smiling produces endorphins: McKenna, P . (2010). *I Can Make You Confident.* Sterling. 89. (Brain change in two months smiling produces endorphins that make the body feed good smiling releases serotonin –a happy neurotransmitter into the blood stream.)

Chapter 8 Learning to Problem Solve

93 Consult their brains about what they already know: Schuster, D. (Nov 2012). Brain imagery and problem solving. *American Psychologist* , 603 (Brain uses information stored in brain to solve problems.)

93 Example of Using Knowledge: Mellers, B., Stone, E., Pavel A., Rohrbaugh, N., Emlen, Metz, E. Ungar L., Bishop M. M., Horwitz, M., Merkle, E., & Telock, P. (2015).The Psychology of Intelligence Analysis: Drivers of Prediction Accuracy in World Politics, *Journal of Experimental Psychology Applied.* 21, 1-14. (Using knowledge.)

93 *Problem solving is a process to identify, analyze, and solve problems:* (n. n.) (n. d.) Retrieved from https://www.merriam-webster.com/dictionary/problem-solving (Process to find a solution to a problem.)

93 All problem strategies use data: (--back up your hunches with data.) Mellers, B. (January 2016). Using data in problem solving. Esther derby associates. Retrieved from http://www.estherderby.com/2016/01/using-data-in-problem-solving.html

Malouff, J., (n.d.). Over fifty Problem-solving strategies. NUE University of New England. Retrieved from https://www.une.edu.au/about-
230

une/academic-schools/bcss/news-and-events/psychology-community-activities/over-fifty-problem-solving-strategies-explained

93 Loui Pasture once said that: chance favors the prepared mind: Drew, S. (March 2010). ASBMB today. Retrieved from https://www.bing.com/search?q=Loui+Pasture+once+said+that+%E2%80%9C__+chance+favors+the+prepared+mind.%E2%80%9D&form=EDGSPH&mkt=en-us&httpsmsn=1&refig=52ceaef5bcaa454aa84f4e92c964c4ca&sp=-1&pq=undefined&sc=0-65&qs=n&sk=&cvid=52ceaef5bcaa454aa84f4e92c964c4ca (Loui Pasture once said that chance favors the prepared mind.)

95 Then they watched birds: McCullough, D. (2015). *The Wright Brothers*. Simon & Schuster.

95 In 2011 Feng Zang had a problem: he was trying to "edit cells from mammals:" Park, A. *TIME Magazine.* The editor of life's building blocks. Retrieved from *http://time.com/collection-post/4518815/feng-zhang-next-generation-leaders/*

96 A problem-solving strategy is a method to achieve some objective: Anthony, L., **&** Chron. (2018 Herst). Goal setting, problem solving and learning. Chron. Retrieved from http://educservtech.com/Goal%20Setting%20and%20Problem%20Solving.pdf

97 Edison did when trying to find how to develop a more effective incandescent electric light: Furr, N. (June 9, 2011). Forbs.com. (How failure taught Edison.)

**97 *There is a pattern or structure to our world: (n. n.. (n. d.). Teacher Vision.* Retrieved from https://www.teachervision.com/problem-solving-find-pattern

98 It was found that the group with the instruction on finding structure to their lessons had increased scores on tests of creativity: Dickinson, D. J. (1967) Doctoral dissertation. Oklahoma State University. The effects of practice in making classifications on achievement and intelligence.

99 Working backward: Bethany (n.n.). (March 2018)). Math Greek Mama. Retrieved from https://mathgeekmama.com/problem-solving-by-working-backwards/

101 *Solving problems of prediction with the average rule:* Christian, B. & Griffiths, T. (2016). *Algorithms to Live By.* Henry Holt and Company. 135

102 A Harvard University psychologist, Deirdre Barrett, found that when students were given a problem to dream about, nearly half of the students did dream about the problem: Barrett, D. (n. d.). Retrieved from https://www.revolvy.com/topic/Deirdre%20Barrett&item_type=topic. The roadmap to modern IT Operations, Deirdre Barrett, also in *Monitor on Psychology.*

103 Sleep can also have an impact on students' grades. Kids making getting 15 minutes or more of sleep get higher grades than those making B's. Kids making B get 15 minutes or more of sleep than those making C's: Eurka A. (n. d.). American Academy of sleep medicine. Retrieved from thttps://www.eurekalert.org/pub_releases/2008-06/aaos-psc050708.php. (Poor sleep can affect a student's grades.)

103 Rules *to Problem Solving:* Billstein, L, & Lott. S. (n.d.). *Science.* 4 steps to problem solving. Science World. Retrieved from http://teacher.scholastic.com/lessonrepro/lessonplans/steppro.htm Billstein, Libeskind, and Lott have adopted these problem solving steps in their book "*A Problem Solving Approach to Mathematics for Elementary School Teachers.* (The Benjamin/Cummings Publishing Co. (They are based on the problem-solving steps first outlined by George Polya in 1945.
Understanding the problem
Devising a plan
Carrying out the plan
Looking back)

105 A baseline of their work would also be helpful. Hampton, C., Berkowityz, B., & Nagy, K. (n. d.) Community Tool Box. Developing baseline measures. Retrieved from http://ctb.ku.edu/en/table-of-contents/assessment/assessing-community-needs-and-resources/developing-baseline-measures/main (A baseline is a measure taken before they start their problem-solving program.)

Chapter 9 Learning to use Problem-Solving Coping

108 *Coping is a method of responding to frustration or a blocked goal*. (n. n.). (n. d.). *Your Dictionary. Cope*. Retrieved from http://www.yourdictionary.com/cope "--manage something difficult or challenging."

108 Problem solving coping emotional coping: Lazarus, R. S., & Folkman, S. (1984*). Stress, appraisal and coping*. New York: Springer.

109 In 2014 the *New York Times* published a story about a youngster who was autistic: Charleston, B. (2014). *New York Times*. Opinion Page. Retrieved from http://www.nytimes.com/2013/05/23/opinion/defining-my-own-dyslexia.html?_r=0 (Blake Charleston, describes what it is like to grow up with a disability such as being autistic)

111 Dr. Jann Cupp, coauthor of the *Academic and Social Coping Inventory:* Cupp, J. (1993). The relationship of Academic and Social Coping to Achievement and Adaptability. Unpublished doctoral dissertation, The University of Tennessee.

112 Those who blame others are more likely to get in difficulty again: people who are released from prison are more likely to commit crimes if they use the coping strategy of blaming others: George Mason University Psychology Science. (March 2014). cited in *Monitor on Psychology*. 45, 23.

113 An unpublished study by Michelle Dawson, Lorie Beller, Lynn Churchman, and Karen Loy: Dawson, Michelle, Beller, L., Churchman, L., & Loy, K. (1997). The University of Tennessee, Department of Educational and Counseling Psychology.

113 This is sometimes referred to as self-regulation: Mahoney,M. (1974). Cognition and Behavior Modification. Ballinger Publishing Company, Cambridge, Mass., 215. (Perceived control may be a more significant factor in coping with stress than the actual implementation of controlling options.)

113 You can use information from the Brain Works *Project* at: (n. n).
(1999-2018). GoDaddy. Brain Works Project. Retrieved from
http://copingskills4kids.net/Brain_Works_Project.html (for more
information, including pictures on how the brain works in coping with
stress.)

115 Self-Talk with Blocked Goals Self instructional training: Ibid.
Mahoney, M. (1974). *Cognition and Behavior Modification, Ballinger
Publishing Company*, Cambridge, Mass. Belief, Counter-Control, and
Choice. 227-252. "Belief is a rule of action—." 229.

115 Another way to teach coping is to use scenarios: (n. n.). (n. d.) BU.
Center for Teaching & Learning. Retrieved from
http://www.bu.edu/ctl/teaching-resources/using-case-studies-to-teach/

118 Problem solving steps: (n. n.). (n. d.) Excerpter from Beecroft, B. D.,
Grace L., Duffy G. L., & John W. Moran, J. W. *The Executive Guide to
improvement and Change.* ASO Learn about quality. Retrieved from
http://asq.org/learn-about-quality/problem-solving/overview/overview.html

Chapter 10 Learning Self Management

**123 With self-management your students will be determining the
goals, how to pursue them, and their own rewards, not someone else's**:
(n .n). (2005). dictionary.com Retrieved from
http://www.dictionary.com/browse/self-management (self control.)

**123 (contingency) An agreement with your youngsters that if they
make the desired response:** (n. n.) (n.d.). *Merriam Webster*. Retrieved
from https://www.merriam-webster.com/dictionary/contingent

**125 But how many people who make a New Year's resolution actually
succeed? But how many people who make a New Year's resolution**:
Diamond, D. (January 2013). Forbs. Pharman & Health care. Just 8% of
People Achieve their New Year's Resolution. Retrieved from
https://www.forbes.com/sites/dandiamond/2013/01/01/just-8-of-people-
achieve-their-new-years-resolutions-heres-how-they-did-it/#cb5741a596b2
(Just 8% achieve their goal.)

127 She used simulation to turn around an important game: ESPN.
(April 2012). The stuff legions are made of. Retrieved from

http://www.espn.com/womens-college-basketball/story/_/id/7829139/pat-summitt-milestone-wins (Pat Head Summitt.)

Duhigg, C. (2012). *The Power of Habit*. Random House, New York. P110-1112. (Visualizations of perfect race Michael Phelps. Swimming Coach Bob Bowman.)

126 Simulation is approximating the real thing in a form of covert practice: (n. n.). (February 12, 2016.) *National Geographic*. Your Brain. 79 (Merely thinking---brains acts just as just as they would if you had actually gotten up . . . .)

127 Your brain acts as if the simulation is real: Scimeca, D. (April 2016). The Kernel Retrieved from https://kernelmag.dailydot.com/issue-sections/features-issue-sections/16348/virtual-reality-psychology/

127 Students will monitor how they are doing before they start their program (called a baseline.). (n,n,). (n.d.). Retrieved from https://www.bing.com/search?q=baseline&form=EDGSPH&mkt=en-us&httpsmsn=1&refig=b34f20dda9184cb997046dc333251f88&sp=-1&ghc=1&pq=baseline&sc=8-8&qs=n&sk=&cvid=b34f20dda9184cb997046dc333251f88

128 A cue can be anything that signals a behavior to occur: Donath, J. (n. d.). Signals, cues, and meaning. Retrieved from http://smg.media.mit.edu/papers/Donath/SignalsTruthDesign/SignalsCues AndMeaning.pdf

128 Also having to write how you are doing based on data will help you to be objective about your progress and make you feel responsible. Travers, C. (September 2017) *Monitor on Psychology*. 57.

130 Use a public display of progress: People who make a public display of their progress toward a goal do better than those who do not make their progress public. People who are trying to lose weight lose more when they post how they're doing. Parents especially should see a record of progress. (n. n.). (Oct 2015). Retrieved from https://www.sciencedaily.com/releases/2015/10/151029101349.htm

131 *Using the stickers as cues to think positively:* McKenna, P. (2010). *I Can Make You Confident*. Sterling, New York, /London (achieve goal

brain lights up serotonin –brain's happy chemical. 119 (cites a study where depressed participants were given colored stickers to put around.)

Chapter 11 Learning Self-Management Rules

133 Charles Darwin made a list of advantages: Charles Darwin made a list of advantages and disadvantages: Christian, B & Griffiths, T. (2016). *Algorithms to Live By*, Henry Holt and Company. *149.*

136 We know that students who were asked to write about positive experiences for three consecutive days, three months later, had fewer visits to the health clinic and more positive moods: Clair, J. (2018). How positive thinking builds your skills, boosts your health, and improves your work. News Letter. Retrieved from https://jamesclear.com/positive-thinking

Chapter 12 Learning to Think Critically

145 *Prescribed to preposterous beliefs* The Witches **Stacy 9, in her book the** *Witches:* Schiff, S. (2015). *The Witches*. Back Bay Books/ Little Brown and Company, Hatcher Book Group. 9.

145 Around 75% of teachers: Hurd, P. (2004). The foundation for critical thinking. Retrieved from http://www.criticalthinking.org/pages/the-state-of-critical-thinking-today/523

149 Children who move: Darling, N.. (July 11, 2010). *Psychology Today*. Moving is tough for kids. *Monitor on Psychology*. Retrieved from https://www.psychologytoday.com/blog/thinking-about-kids/201007/moving-is-tough-kids (Children who move from one town to another.)

149 *Federal Trade Commission, Consumer Information* **on the internet:** (n. n.). (n. d.). Consumer Information. Retrieved from https://www.consumer.ftc.gov/

150 Source of information: Jones, K. (December 2017). Reliable sources: promoting critical thinking in the (mis)informational age.

Retrieved from https://www.facultyfocus.com/articles/teaching-and-learning/promoting-critical-thinking-misinformation-age/

154 Listen, here's one from *Scientific American* saying that a study showed that eating cooked carrots for six weeks help bring night vision up to normal: Fine-Moran, D. (n. d.). Retrieved from https://www.scientificamerican.com/article/fact-or-fiction-carrots-improve-your-vision/

155 Charles Dickens' book (n. n.). (*Great Expectations* published as a weekly from 1860 to 1861.) Wikipedia. Great Expectations. Retrieved from https://en.wikipedia.org/wiki/Great_Expectations

155 Inductive reasoning: Rouse, M. (1999-2018). Retrieved from https://whatis.techtarget.com/definition/inductive-reasoning

156 Inductive reasoning a conclusion of an argument may be probably, based on the evidence: (n.n.). (May 2018 revised). Wikipedia. Inductive Reasoning. Retrieved from https://en.wikipedia.org/wiki/Inductive_reasoning

Chapter 13 Learning About Obstacles

157 Reasoning a conclusion Thinking: (n. n.). (n. d.). Retrieved from http://www.studymode.com/essays/Barriers-And-Obstacles-To-Critical-Thinking-1026012.html

159 Your brain is already wired to go with the "thinking habits" you already have: Alvermann, D. (2013). *TIME Magazine*. Learning from mistakes is harder than we think. Retrieved from http://ideas.time.com/2013/04/29/learning-from-mistakes-is-harder-than-we-think/at the (Study after study shows that "students ignored correct textual information when it conflicted with their previously held concepts."

157 When someone found the large tooth and tusk of a mastodon: Kolbert, E. (2016). *The Sixth Extinction.* Picador Henry Holt and Company New York.

159 At one time scientists believed that animals and plants that existed in their time had always existed and changed little over time: Kolbert,

E. (2014). *The Sixth Extinction.* Picador Henry Holt and Company, New York. 38-41.

162   When a survey was conducted it was found that most people approved of this if it is described as "end of life support" but they showed less approval if the message was described as "assisted suicide." O'Neill, S. (June 4, 2015). KPCC Health. Assisted suicide or aid in dying? Retrieved from http://www.scpr.org/news/2015/06/04/52187/assisted-suicide-or-aid-in-dying-the-semantic-batt/ (Framing means contriving the *context* of information.)

163 Professor Elizabeth Loftis' research shows how memory distortion can happen to most of us in problem solving: Loftus, Elizabeth F. (Post 9/11 AP Sept 2001). Intelligence Gathering. *Monitor on Psychology.* 66, 532-541. (Example of gist and bleeding.)

161 Garrison Keillor, speaking on National Public Radio:: (July 27, 2013). *The News from Lake Wobegon* ..... Saturday, July 14 2012 11:00 PM ..... Retrieved from broadcasting the finest programs from NPR and Public Radio International,. Prairie Home Companion. (Example of embellishment.)

162 In his book, *How We Decide*, cites studies in which participants who were stressed were asked to note when they saw a blinking light in their peripheral field: Lehrer, J. *How We Decide.* Mariner Books, Houghton Mifflin Harcourt, Boston, New York. 209. (Studies in which participants who were stressed were asked to note when they saw a blinking light in their peripheral field.)

162 David DiSalvo describes a study: DiSalvo, D. (2011). *What makes your brain happy and why you should do the opposite.* Prometheus Books. 35.

163 Elizabeth Loftis article published in *Memory* and reviewed in the *Monitor on Psychology* about one-third of the participants recalled false memories like taking hot air balloon rides: (n. n). (March 2017). *Monitor on Psychology(* about one-third of the participants recalled false memories like taking hot air balloon rides and playing pranks on other— and they could remember the details.) 12.

168 Attitude is critical to your thinking and the thinking of your students: Paul, R. W. & Elder, L. (2002) *Critical Thinking: Tools for Taking Charge of Your Professional and Personal Life, Person Education, Inc.* Upper Saddle River, NJ.

Matthew J. Hornsey, M. J. & Felding, K. S. (July-August 2017). Attitude Roots and Jiu Jitsu Persuasion: Understanding and overcoming the Motivated Rejection of Science *American Psychologist* ,429-473. (Group activates work best.)

166 But you can control your emotions: According to Compas, B. E., J. K. Connor-Smith, J. K., Saltzman H., Thomsen, A. H. & Wadsworth, M. E. (2001). Coping with stress during childhood and adolescence: problems, progress, and potential in theory and research. *Psychological Bulletin.* 2001. 87-127. (Coping responses involve *efforts*, often under a person's control, to manage thoughts,)

166 Often under a person's control to manage thought, emotions, and behavior: Levy, D. J. (2016). Disparities in Educational Outcomes. *American Psychologist.* 71, 455-473

Chapter 14 Leaning Rules to Think Critically

168 If your attitude is "closed: Paul, R. W. (2002). *Critical Thinking: Tools for Taking Charge of Your Professional and Personal Life, Person Education*, Inc. Upper Saddle River, NJ

170 When judges' rulings dealing with women: Liptak, Adam. (June 2014). https://www.nytimes.com/2014/06/17/us/judges-with-daughters-more-often-rule-in-favor-of-womens-rights.html

171 Almost everyone said the Wright brothers were "crazy" to try to fly like a bird: McCullough, D. (2016)). *The Wright Brothers.* Simon and Schuster.

171 According to Yuval Harari in his book *Homo Deus:* Harari, Y. N. (2016). *Homo Deus. A brief history of tomorrow. Vintage.* 24-36.

170 Glenn Curtiss: McCullough, D. (2016). *The Wright Brothers*, Simon and Schuster.

171 Talking about themselves: Costello, M. (May 2012). Retrieved from https://www.cbsnews.com/news/study-talking-about-yourself-online-provides-similar-brain-reward-as-sex-eating/

171 Another example of reframing is one mentioned in *TIME Magazine* in January 2017: (n. n.). (January 2017). *TIME Magazine.* (Students who are anxious over an exam have been told that the anxiety causes them to be more alert and motivated.)

172 Stanford neurobiologist Robert Sapolsky: Sapolsky, R. (August/September 2007). Being emotional has been shown to make you less empathic. When your brain has a mind of its own Q&A *AARP*, 28-29

173 According to Bruce E. Compas, Jennifer K. Connor-Smith, Heidi Saltzman, Alexandra Harding Thomsen, and Martha E. Wadsworth writing in the *Psychological Bulletin:* Compas, B. E. et al. (2014). 114. (Open minded means recognizing you are biased.)

(n. n.). (n. d.). WIKI. How to overcome unconscious and hidden biases. Retrieved from https://www.wikihow.com/Overcome-Unconscious-and-Hidden-Biases. (Six steps.)

173 Now physicians in training are using reframing: Robertson, I. (January 12, 2017). *TIME Magazine.* !89. (Reframing what doctors do when faced with the death of a patient.)

173 TME Magazine: Robertson, I. (January 12, 2017). *Time Magazine. How stressing out can help you succeed. 189.* (Reframing telling children that having stress increased motivation and attention.).

175 Sleep causes you to moderate your emotional experiences—it flattens them: *National Geographic.* Your brain. (2016).

Perry, B. D. (2013). Retrieved from http://teacher.scholastic.com/professional/bruceperry/brainlearns.htm April 25 (Sleep helps consolidate memories.)

175 President Harry Truman: Poen, M. (1999). *Strictly Confidential and Personal.* https://www.goodreads.com/book/show/865059.Strictly_Personal_and_Confidential. (The letter Harry Truman wrote and never mailed.)

175 When you self-monitor you talk to yourself, telling yourself what to do and questioning yourself whether you have done what you are supposed to do: Novotney, A. (January 2016). *Monitor on Psychology.* (Frequently monitoring and public reporting progress toward goals increases the chance of success. University of Sheffield,. *Psychology Bulletin*, online Oct 19.)

176 Federal Trade Commission, Consumer Affairs: (n. n.). (n. d.). Consumer Information. Retrieved from https://www.consumer.ftc.gov/

Chapter 15 Leaning to be Open Minded

178 What is being open-minded? Herford Z. (n.d.) *Essential Life Skills.* Have an open mind. Retrieved from https://www.essentiallifeskills.net/openmind.html

178 open minded means recognizing you are biased: (n. n.). (n. d.). WIKI. How to overcome unconscious and hidden biases. Retrieved from https://www.wikihow.com/Overcome-Unconscious-and-Hidden-Biases (Six steps.)

179 In a study published in 2013 by Uiel Haran, Ilans Ritov, & Barbara A. Mellers to determine if people who are open minded could predict uncertain qualities: Haran,U., Ritov, I., & Mellers, B. A. (May 2013). *Judgment and Decision Making.* 4 (3), 188-201

179 In a study: Kurglanski, A. W., & Webster, D. M. (1996**).** Motivated closing of the mind: "seizing and freezing." *Psychological Review.* 103, 263-283. (Example: I am one who prefers to know one big thing.)

180 Here's how a study by Barbara Mellers and associates from the University of Pennsylvania and Missouri published in 2015 that tested whether open-minded individuals can make more accurate predictions than closed-minded individuals about geopolitical events. Mellers, B., Stone, E., Pavel A., Rohrbaugh, N., Emlen, Metz, E. Ungar L., Bishop M. M., Horwitz, M., Merkle, E., & Telock, P. (2015).The Psychology of Intelligence Analysis: Drivers of Prediction Accuracy in World Politics, *Journal of Experimental Psychology Applied,* 2015. .21, 1-14.

180 **Perseverance increases over intelligence as a predictor of grades:** Goleman, D. (October, 1995). *Emotional Intelligence.* Bantam Book.

182 **According to Leo Widrich writing in *Buffer Social*, by simply telling a story we can plant ideas, thoughts, and emotion into the listeners' brains.** Widrich, L. (n. d.). Retrieved from https://blog.bufferapp.com/science-of-storytelling-why-telling-a-story-is-the-most-powerful-way-to-activate-our-brains

182 **Studies have shown that when students go off to college and meet a new clan:** Coles, J. T., Carstens, B. A., Wright, J. M., & Williams, R. L. (2015) Political incongruity between students' ideological identity and a stance on specific policies in a predominately white southern state institution. *Innovative Higher Education*, 40, 5-18.

183 **Sometime between 30,000 and 70,000 years ago a mutation change the brain:** Harari Y. N. (2016). *Saipan: A Brief History of Humankind.* Vintage, *122.*

184 **according to TIMES' Katy Steinmetz because false stories get tweeted six times as fast as true ones**: Steinmetz, K. *TIME Magazine* August 20, 2018, 28-31

187 **Who invented the electric light?** Palermor, E. (August 2017). *Live Science.* Who invented the electric light bulb? ((Federick de Moleyns, Joseph Swan, and J. W. Starr.)
Retrieved from http://articles.latimes.com/2004/nov/01/opinion/oe-evans1
(Before that magical moment in October 1879, Edison had worked out no fewer than 3,000 theories about electric light, each of them reasonable and apparently likely to be true -- but in only two cases did his experiments work.)

187 **There is enough water in Lake Superior:** Snyder, M. (March 2012). 40 Weird facts about the United States. Retrieved from http://theeconomiccollapseblog.com/archives/40-weird-facts-about-the-united-states-that-are-almost-too-crazy-to-believe

187 **it's almost impossible to understand someone who has a different view:** Paul, Richard W. & Elder, Linda. (2002). *Critical Thinking: Tools*

for Taking Charge of Your Professional and Personal Life, Person Education, Inc. Upper Saddle River, NJ.

189 WWI the French had planned to attack the Germans: Tuchman, Barbara. (1990). *The Guns of August.* Ballantine Books, New York.

191 Reasoning is a skill just like that of comprehending: Fisher, A. (2011)). *Critical Thinking.* Understanding reasoning: different patterns of reasoning. Cambridge University Press. 35-49.

191 Reasoning—cause and effect: Pearl, J. (n. d.). Reasoning with cause and effect. Retrieved from http://bayes.cs.ucla.edu/IJCAI99/ijcai-99.pdf (Causal events cause a behavior or another event to follow,)

Chapter 16 Think Critically and to Reason

191 Deductive reasoning: Fisher, A. (2011)). *Critical Thinking.* Understanding reasoning: different patterns of reasoning. Cambridge University Press. 35-49.

Paul, R. W. & Elder, L. (2002). *Critical Thinking: Tools for Taking Charge of Your Professional and Personal Life, Person Education, Inc.* Upper Saddle River, NJ.

Rouse, M. (1999-2018). Whatis.com Retrieved from http://whatistechtarget.com/definition/deductive-reasoning (What Is Deductive reasoning is a logical process in which a conclusion is based on the concordance of multiple premises that are generally assumed to be true.)

(n. n.). (June 2005). Butte College. Deductive, Inductive and adductive reasoning. Deductive reasoning general rule If x=4. And y = 1 then 2X+1y= 9. Retrieved from https://www.butte.edu/departments/cas/tipsheets/thinking/reasoning.html

Changing Minds. Types of reasoning. (n. n). (n. d.). Poen, M. M. (1999). http://changingminds.org/disciplines/argument/types_reasoning/types_reas oning.htm (Number of different types of reasoning.)

(n.n.). (n/d.). Ways of Knowing. Type of reasoning. Retrieved from http://hcom301.com/types-of-reasoning.html. (reasoning by comparing to a similar)

(n. n.). (n. d.). Retrieved from https://www.bing.com/images/search?q=types+of+inductive+logic&qpvt=Types+of+inductive+logic&FORM=IGRE

195 Preschoolers appear to learn math best when they're taught using brightly colored or unusually textured objects that are unfamiliar to them, according to research conducted by psychologists at the University of Notre Dame: (July 2013). Monitor on Psychology. In Brief. Preschoolers appear to learn math best when they're taught using brightly colored or unusually textured objects. . Retrieved from http://www.apa.org/monitor/2013/07-08/inbrief.aspx (First published in the *Journal of Child Development*, and was conducted by faculty at the *University of Notre Dame*,)

195 When you don't have explicit information (you did not see, hear, or feel the event) you will likely use some form of inductive logic: Retrieved from http://www.occonline.occ.cccd.edu/online/gmonahan/types%20of%20reasoning.pdf

195 An inference is coming to some kind of conclusion based on your past experience and the information given to you when the information is not explicit (you don't directly see it): (n. n.). (n. d.). Vocabulary.com. https://www.vocabulary.com/dictionary/inference.

Chapter 17 Monitor Thinking, Scenarios

203 A scenario is a postulated series of events: (n .n.). (n. d.). Scenario. . Retrieved from https://www.bing.com/search?q=defination++scenario+&form=EDGSPH&mkt=en-us&httpsmsn=1&refig=890047a6d4e3417b9e1ff4c5e2262c44&sp=-1&pq=defination+scenario+&sc=2-20&qs=n&sk=&cvid=890047a6d4e3417b9e1ff4c5e2262c44

Trujillo-J. L. (2014). Faculty Focus. Retrieved from https://www.facultyfocus.com/articles/effective-teaching-strategies/guiding-students-think-critically-using-case-studies/ (Using a scenario-based story to help student to deepen their understanding of a concept.)

205 Our drinking water is dirty: (n. n). (n. d.). Retrieved from http://www.mindbodygreen.com/0-13217/why-you-simply-must-filter-your-water.html (The *Environmental Working Group* has found that 85% of our drinking water is filled with as many as 300 contaminants.)

205 You might want to also look at this web site: Ipman, F. (n. d.). Why you simply must filter your water. Mindbodygreen. Retrieved from http://www.mindbodygreen.com/0-13217/why-you-simply-must-filter-your-water.html (for more information on drinking water.)

206 You should want your students to monitor their thinking: (n. n.) (January 2016). Monitor in Psychology. Frequently monitoring and public reporting progress toward goals increases the chance of success. University of Sheffield Participants who were prompted to monitor their progress were more likely to achieve their goals. Participants who recorded or publicly reported their monitoring has even more success. *Psychological Bulletin*, online Oct 19.) 27.

About the Author

Dr. Donald Dickinson is professor emeritus from the University *of Tennessee, Department of Educational and Counseling Psychology.* He received his Bachelor, Masters, and Doctoral degrees from Oklahoma State University.

He was employed as a school psychologist five years before becoming the Coordinator of Student Services for the Clark County School District in Las Vegas for seven years. He was an instructor at UNLV while living in Las Vegas.

At the University of Tennessee, he was Director or Co-Director of the School Psychology Program for most of his tenure there. Most of his publications were on the cognitive functions of learning which is covered in the chapter on Learning Deeper Comprehension in this book. He has also several publications on behavior modification. For many years, he and his students conducted parent-training programs, teaching parents how to assist in helping their children to learn.

He married Teresa Ann Miller of Nashville, Tennessee and will have spent 63 years with her as of November 22 of 2018. He has two delightful daughters, one a special- education teacher and the other an attorney. He has four very talented grandchildren and four wonderful great-grandchildren.

www.ingramcontent.com/pod-product-compliance
Lightning Source LLC
LaVergne TN
LVHW051624080426
835511LV00016B/2165